Austro-Hungarian Infantry
1914 - 1918

J. S. Lucas

ALMARK PUBLISHING CO. LTD., LONDON

©1973, Almark Publishing Co. Ltd.

Text © J. S. Lucas; Art work © Matthew Cooper

All rights reserved. No part of this publication may be reproduced, stored in a retrieval system, or transmitted by any means, electronic, mechanical or by photo copying without prior permission from the publishers.

First published—January 1973

ISBN 0 85524096 2 (hard cover edition)

ISBN 0 85524097 0 (paper covered edition)

Printed in Great Britain by
The Byron Press Ltd., 59 Palmerston Road, Wealdstone, Middlesex
for the publishers, Almark Publishing Co. Ltd.,
270 Burlington Road, New Malden, Surrey KT3 4NL, England

Author's Dedication

The Army of Austria-Hungary broke up and vanished into history during November, 1918. With the passing of time, less and less is remembered of a Force which played a major, and sometimes a dominant role in Central European history, for nearly three centuries.

This book has been written to commemorate, generally, the infantrymen who fought in the 'last war of the last Kaiser', but is dedicated specifically to my late father-in-law, Lieutenant Josef Anton Schranz, sometime of the Imperial and Royal Infantry Regiment, No 88, holder of the Silver Medal for Bravery.

Acknowledgments

The author and illustrator wish to acknowledge, with grateful thanks, the help of the Austrian Heeresgeschichtliches Museum, the Imperial War Museum, London, the War Office Library, London and other official institutions. Our thanks are especially due to the following; Mrs Rosemary Sharman, David Nash, David Bradley, Cyril McCann, Laurie Milner, Brian Davies and Peter Chamberlain, all of whom gave us expert advice and invaluable help. Particular thanks go to Herr L. Klein for allowing us to use his source material and some of the photographs in his collection.

BELOW: His Imperial Majesty Franz Josef 1st, Emperor-King. FRONT COVER: Ensign, Common Army Infantry Regiment No 18 with regimental colour; Arms of the Austro-Hungarian Empire. BACK COVER: Private Soldier, Common Army Infantry Regiment No 41. Field Service Order with aiguillettes for a marksman 2nd class; General-Major, Field Service Dress, 1914.

Introduction

THE armies of the Austro-Hungarian Empire which went into the Field for the Great War of 1914 were the heirs and successors of men who had defeated the Turks at Vienna, had given Napoleon's forces their first European setback and had, in wars and campaigns since the fifteenth century, secured for themselves a military reputation of which they could be justifiably proud.

A study of history shows that small and energetic nations who, by conquest, trade or marriage obtain dominion over other more heavily populated states eventually reach a stage in their development when, their own population being too small in number to supply both an expanding Civil Service as well as an army large enough to defend the State, they must recruit their soldiers from among subject peoples who may be of low military ability or of doubtful loyalty.

The growth of the Austrian Empire by expansion into Central, Southern and Eastern Europe soon faced the Habsburg government with the problem of manning the regiments and to the men of the Germanic peoples who had, at one time, formed the bulk of the Austrian Army had been added the men recruited from the eleven or twelve racial groups which made up the Dual Monarchy. The results of the application by the Imperial government to this problem eventually brought the Army to a point at which only 28 per cent of its total strength was native Austrian/German. Nearly one half (44 per cent) of the whole was Slav and 18 per cent Hungarian, with the Rumanian and Italian peoples of the Empire contributing 8 per cent and 2 per cent respectively. There were pronounced differences between the mental levels of the races within the Dual Monarchy and a higher proportion of the more intelligent Hungarian, Czech and German peoples was to be found in the Cavalry, the Artillery and the technical branches of the Army than in the Infantry; 67 per cent of whose total strength was made up of Slavs.

The Habsburg Monarchy, like some other Empires, contained ethnic groups which were racially or religiously antipathetic. It is unlikely that this racial hostility needed to be deliberately fomented by the Austrian government as an application of the 'divide and rule' principle. The Magyar hatred and oppression of its Slav minorities, to give just one example, was an international scandal. The inability or the unwillingness of the various national groups to tolerate each other would, perhaps, have been almost impossible of resolution under any other form of government than a Monarchy and the Austrian solution to this problem had been a simple, almost feudal, but very effective one; direct and personal loyalty to the Emperor who, as Head of the Army, was himself a soldier. The loyalty of the Army was focussed upon and centred around the person of the Monarch, representing the traditional Dynasty, and all ranks of the Armed Forces were deeply aware of the affection in which the ruling family held them. This two-way loyalty, from the Army to the Sovereign and from him back to them, this paternalism, permeated the whole military structure and was reflected in the officers' treatment of their men.

ABOVE: Newly commissioned officers, from all branches of the Armed Forces, at the end of their passing-out parade. Note the officer second from right who is a member of a Tyrolean Kaiserjäger regiment.

Habsburg recruited for its military service the volunteer, professional soldier and replaced any racial or religious differences vis-a-vis his comrades in the barrack room with the twin mystiques of an Emperor, in the devotion to whose person they were as one, and of the Regiment, which became the Nation, the religion and the family of them all. It was this feudal loyalty which held the Empire together for centuries and only in the latter half of the nineteenth century did the bonds begin to loosen.

To officer his Armies the Emperor did not choose men from only the traditional warrior families. In order that the military should not become a nation within the nation, he selected leaders from the widest possible social and national structure of the people of his Empire, although one third of the professional, officer class was commissioned from the Austro/German nation. This broad based group, by virtue of postings to every province of the Empire, was a cosmopolitan one and was in touch with attitudes and aspirations of all the component nations, but chiefly was it influenced by the social habits and the culture of the Imperial capital—Vienna. As a result of these influences the Austrian Army was officered by a more intelligent, humane and sophisticated type of man than it was usual to find in the service of the Prussian state or the German Reich. Indeed, it was essential to the Austrian officer's success as a leader that he be so, for among the men whom he might have to command were such diverse types as volatile Italians, intelligent Czechs or primitive Ruthenians.

Austria's defeat at the hands of the Prussians in 1866 led to the first of a series of army reorganisations and the most important of these, undertaken soon after that war, was the introduction of general, military conscription. This move destroyed the Army of long-term, professional soldiers and replaced it by tides of short-service men, who were still civilian at heart, and who brought politics, nationalism and even pacifism into the barrack room.

One early concession to nationalistic demands was the use of national languages. In the early days of the Empire attempts had been made at establishing some kind of uniformity of language in the polyglot army and there had

ABOVE: The Archduke Friedrich during a tour of inspection on the Rumanian Front. At the date of this photograph the Archduke was Commander-in-Chief of the Austro-Hungarian forces. The officer behind him is the German commander von Falkenhayn. Note the ADC on the left wearing goggles, having just alighted from the staff car. (IWM-Q23995).

grown up an unofficial but widely used patois, Army Slav. Each recruit was taught a basic, eighty German words of command and frequently learned to speak and understand the Imperial language. German it was hoped would be more than the language of command and should serve as an instrument of unification. The charge that it was used to 'Germanise' the subject nations cannot be substantiated: indeed it would be true to say that its use was not enforced to the degree that might have been expected, given the need for easier inter-provincial communication. In the new armies the language of instruction depended upon the racial composition of the regiment. Unintegrated units were taught in their native tongue; indeed, any unit having more than 20 per cent of its total strength in one racial group was permitted to have instruction in that language.

But more serious than the language question was the demand made by the Hungarians for their own Army, and the Imperial authorities were forced to concede to the Magyars the right to raise a separate, military force. This Honved, as it was called, needed to be paralleled by a similar, Austrian organisation and, thus, the Landwehr came into being.

Other expressions of national identity had given cause for disquiet even in the old Army and, as early as the Austro-Prussian War, it had been thought tactful to withdraw the Austro/Italian units facing Victor Emmanuel and to deploy them against the Prussians. Methods aimed at preventing disaffection and other than the simple withdrawal of suspect regiments, included the removal of regimental depots from their native areas and postings of units to other parts of the Empire. Integration of men of differing races was introduced and carried through even to battalion level.

But the authorities did not have to combat only the racial stresses and nationalist feelings within the regiments. Other opposition to the Armed Forces and to the military budgets was carried out by civilian, political, 'liberal' circles throughout the Empire, but chiefly in the capital city. To this political hostility was added the fact that numbers raised by conscription were becoming insufficient to meet the increased demands made upon the Services. Despite population growth during the latter half of the nineteenth century there was only a slight rise in the numbers of men available for recruiting. In 1870 with a population of 36,000,000, some 100,000 men had been eligible for military service. In 1910, when the population had risen by fifteen millions to a total of 51,000,000, the number available for the Services had risen by only 26,000.

The Army was, in fact, in great danger of being unable to find enough men to ensure the security of the Empire. The military Establishment in times of peace was less than half a million men and this force, its maintenance, expansion and equipping was paid out of a military budget of just over £22,000,000 (1913/1914 Estimates).

When war came the expansion of the Army to a total figure of 3,350,000, all ranks—which included the Landwehr, the Honved, the Landsturm, the

LEFT: Sentry of the 19th Infantry Common Army Regiment in the trenches. Galicia, 1916. From his highly polished boots it would seem that this was a quiet sector of the line.

ABOVE: Before the trench systems became established infantrymen had individual fox holes. These men are seen beating off a Russian assault during the first offensives on the Eastern Front, September, 1914. They are all carrying the hide knapsack as described in the section on Arms and Equipment.

men of the Ersatz Reserve and 66,000 volunteers was barely sufficient to dispose the military effort of the Empire in a major war on two, and later, on three fronts.

This figure of over three million men may, at first glance appear to be an impressive total but the actual figure of fighting men on active service was 1,421,000. All the rest were rear echelon, supply and medical personnel. Even the Infantry total of 1100 battalions contained 401 battalions which were either Landsturm, Line-of-Communication, reinforcement (Marsch) battalions, or formations moving up to, or leaving the battlefront. Upon mobilisation it was the Reservist who, constituting four fifths of Company strengths, brought these up to War Establishment. A shortage of rifles existed and even the confiscation of weapons made for foreign governments could not completely bridge the gap.

This deficiency meant that Landsturm infantry went into battle equipped with the single shot, 11 mm, Werndl rifle which had been long obsolete and wearing the blue uniform which had been discarded years before. Some, indeed, did not even have this much uniform and wore a black and gold brassard on their arm to show their military status.

At the outbreak of war the Army was in the process of a reorganisation which had been started in 1912 by the Chief of Staff, Conrad von Hötzendorf. His radical proposals had not had time to change the ideas of generations nor to disprove the theories which were successful only on manoeuvres or at Staff war games, It was, therefore, the tradition minded regimental officers, using outdated tactics, whose plans and methods were followed in the opening moves of the War. The principle of attack at any price, the ignorance of the effectiveness of the machine-gun and the artillery as weapons of offence as well as defence, were responsible for heavy, unnecessary and irreplaceable losses in experienced Company officers and NCO's.

Within the first two years of the war, 12·5 per cent of all professional officers had been killed. The figure for professional NCO's was 16·5 per cent and that of Reserve Officers was 31·5 per cent. Of the three thousand officer graduates of the Maria Theresa military academy, one in five was killed and from the youngest age groups this figure increased to one in three. The losses among the most experienced officers and men soon brought the armies to a point where many field officers were not professional soldiers but ex-civilians, who brought into military positions of influence, the political disaffection and racial unrest which the Army had always tried to avert. Although at the outbreak of War the Army had marched without any of the mutinies which had occurred during the partial mobilisation of 1912, nevertheless, even in 1914, some Czech regiments made common cause with, and deserted to the Russians. Local mutinies among soldiers of other races were not infrequent. With the extension of the War, the need to switch troops to and from racially sensitive areas became more and more difficult. When Rumania joined the Entente, Austro/Rumanian contingents could not be used in south-east Europe and, with Italy's entry into the War against the Central Powers soldiers whose homes were in the territories claimed by Rome, could not be used against their Latin brothers. Allied propaganda promised self determination and, to combat this longing for national identity and an increasing war-weariness the Austrian Army set up its own propaganda and counter-propaganda organisation. But the rot had gone too deep and the burden of holding the battle line fell more and more heavily upon the reliable Austro/German and Hungarian regiments. It was not unusual to find, particularly towards the end of the war,

BELOW: Officers of a Common Army regiment breakfasting during the campaign against Serbia, Autumn, 1914. Note the line of commissariat wagons in the background and the officer's infantry pattern sabre stuck in the ground on the right.

ABOVE: Common Army regimental band playing in the rear area of the Eastern Front (Poland), 1915. Note the lack of uniformity of footwear.

units, nominally Slav or Latin, which had an unexpectedly and abnormally high proportion of Magyar or Teuton men in their ranks.

The struggle was maintained by the two dominant partners, until almost the last few weeks of the war. Then, and only then, by a move designed to exert political pressure upon the Imperial authorities in Vienna, the Magyar soldiers who had held and supported Habsburg for generations, were ordered to return home and to leave to fight alone in the Field, the Catholic and Austrian regiments upon whose fighting ability and loyalty the Empire had been created.

CONTENTS

Section	Page
Introduction	4
1: Recruitment	11
2: The Infantry in general	16
3: Infantry Organisation	22
4: Landwehr Organisation	34
5: Honved Organisation	53
6: Uniform	56
7: Arms and Equipment	76
Appendix A	96
Appendix B	102
Appendix C	111
Bibliography	112

1: Recruitment

THE divers races which made up the Habsburg Empire were members of one of three component blocs of the Dual Monarchy. The largest of these was the Austrian Empire proper of fourteen provinces, embracing the traditional Austro/German duchies and archduchies, present day Czechoslovakia, parts of Northern Italy, as well as portions of Jugoslavia, Poland and Rumania. Austria's co-partner was the Kingdom of Hungary, encompassing not only Hungary but part of present day Jugoslavia. The third and smallest part of the Habsburg territories was Bosnia-Herzegovina, administered from Vienna through a Bosnia Bureau.

All the Austrian provinces, some of the Hungarian and the province of Bosnia-Herzegovina had autonomy in matters of education, justice and local affairs and each of them had a provincial parliament. National and Imperial affairs were directed from the two capital cities of the Empire and thus there was a government in Vienna as well as Budapest, each with its own Ministry of Defence controlling its own national, territorial Army. There was also an Imperial Ministry of War which had jurisdiction over the Army common to both partners in the Empire.

On matters of equal concern to both parties there was a Common Budget and the estimates for Common Ministries was voted by 'Delegations' of members drawn, annually, from the Austrian and Hungarian parliaments. In matters relating to their own territorial, military forces (the Landwehr and the Honved), both Ministers of Defence were subject to their respective national 'Delegation'. The various Service grants were, therefore, in the hands of groups of civilians who could, and did, exercise powers of veto. The Minister of Defence in Hungary was responsible to his Government and to Parliament in Budapest but the Austrian Defence Minister was directly responsible only to the Emperor. The Austrian civilian administration with its roots in the Aulic Council, was not as flexible as a military Command and a ponderous, civilian bureaucracy stifled the spirit of initiative which the Army had striven to foster.

The Austro-Hungarian forces were composed, as already stated, mainly of conscripted men. The laws governing recruiting, the exemptions from service, the penalties for non-attendance at the various musters and the stages by which an eligible male became a soldier are numerous and complicated but, in principle, it can be said that, in peacetime, every fit, male citizen of the Empire was liable for duty in the Armed Forces from the year of his 19th birthday until the end of the year of his 42nd birthday.

The organisation which gathered the necessary number of recruits from all the provinces was based upon the 16 Army Corps districts into which the Empire was divided. These districts were sub-divided into 112 recruiting areas, three of which (Trieste, Fiume and Sabenico), were responsible for supplying the Fleet with sailors. The numbers required to make up the annual Services

ABOVE: Newly commissioned officers of a Military Academy taking the oath of allegiance to the Emperor. The Colour shown here is probably the Yellow Infantry Colour illustrated on page 48.

contingent, together with the money for the recruiting machinery, was fixed by law and voted by parliamentary 'Delegations'. The men available for conscription formed about 2 per cent of the population; in number usually less than two hundred thousand.

Under Austrian Law the names of men required to present themselves for the draft were listed by the local authorities and posted in public places and, upon attending a Selection Board, the recruit, if found medically fit, was available for duty. A ballot then decided which men would serve in the Regular Army, which would serve in the parallel organisations of Austrian Landwehr or Hungarian Honved and which, if there were any men surplus to requirement in that recruiting area, would be posted to the Ersatz Reserve. The path of the men in the Regular, Honved or Landwehr regiments was simple and direct; they were ordered to report to their units where they carried out their prescribed two years full time service, passed into the Reserve, with its short periods of training for a further ten years and, from thence into the Landsturm. Here they did no further training but were members of a Force liable for service in time of war. From the Landsturm they were discharged at the age of 42 having fulfilled their military duty to the State. The periods of training for these men were as follows:

Common Army reservists were recalled for three, short periods of training during their 10 years on Reserve. Each of these was of about four weeks in duration.

During their decade of Reserve service the Landwehr man had to perform 20 weeks' of training while the Honved man underwent 25 weeks.

Bosnia-Herzegovina had neither Landsturm nor Landwehr service, but reservists were recalled as First, Second or Third Reserves.

Men who had not been selected to serve in the Common Army, Landwehr or Honved regiments were placed in the Ersatz Reserve which contained certain categories of men who, by virtue of their vocation, eg, as priests or schoolteachers or, by their status as sole dependants of families, were exempt from active military service. Men in the Ersatz Reserve were available, if required, for full time duty until the end of their 33rd year, whereupon they passed into the Landsturm until their discharge from further military obligation at the age of 42. These Ersatz Reservists were given certain, very short periods of basic military training and cadres were maintained around which supplementary battalions or Companies of the local regiment could be formed in time of war.

Thus it can be seen that the whole of the military life of an Austrian male, in peacetime, can be divided into two clearly defined parts. Firstly 'active', that is on full time service with a unit of the Regular Army or the two parallel organisations Landwehr and Honved. Secondly 'reservist', either as a member of the Ersatz, Regular Army, Landwehr or Honved reserve and, then in the Landsturm.

The Landsturm, into which all passed, was therefore, a pool of men whose ages ranged from 23 to 42 and who were at varying levels of military competence. There were no facilities for peacetime training and, appreciating that the men in the upper age groups could neither be as fit nor as military effective as the younger men, the authorities divided the Landsturm into two drafts. The men of the First Draft were the younger, more recently trained and were kept in the First Draft until the age of 33. They then automatically became

BELOW: Men of the 39th Common Army, Infantry Regiment marching through a Polish village. Note the regimental colour which accompanied all Regiments on active service until this practice was discontinued during 1916. Note also that some of the men have puttees and others jackboots.

Second Draft until the expiry of their 42nd year when they were discharged from further military obligation.

Officers for the Army were normally professional soldiers who had graduated from one of the Cadet Schools or Military Academies of the Empire. The exceptions to this were those who entered by virtue of their service as One Year Volunteers and who then elected to join the Regular or Landwehr services. These One Year Volunteers were usually middle class students who

The 16 Army Corps Districts of the Dual Monarchy

No	Area covered	Headquarters
I	Western Galicia, Silesia and North Moravia	Cracow
II	Lower Austria, Southern Moravia	Vienna
III	Styria, Carinthia, Carniola, Trieste, Gorizia and Gradisca	Graz
IV	Central Hungary	Budapest
V	Western Hungary	Pozsony
VI	Northern Hungary	Kassa
VII	Eastern Hungary (to west boundary of Transylvania)	Temesvar
VIII	South western Bohemia	Prague
IX	North eastern Bohemia	Leitmeritz
X	Central Galicia	Przemysl
XI	Eastern Galicia and Bukovina	Lemberg
XII	Transylvania	Nagyszeben
XIII	Croatia, Slavonia and Fiume	Agram (Zabreb)
XIV	Tirol, Vorarlberg, Upper Austria and Salzburg	Innsbruck
XV	Bosnia	Sarajevo
XVI	Herzegovina	Ragusa

undertook to feed, clothe and equip themselves for the single year period of their voluntary enlistment. By this service they avoided the need to serve the full term of conscription. Such volunteers were usually found in the technical, administrative or medical branches of the Army.

There were 14 Cadet Schools and these supplied the regiments of the Common Army with non-commissioned ensigns who were gazetted as subaltern officers after two years' service with a regiment. Eleven Cadet Schools supplied officers for the Regular Army; three for the Honved/Landwehr. Two of these three schools were in Hungary, the third in Austria.

One of the four military Academies produced officers for the Common Army infantry and cavalry regiments, a second officers for the technical services, while the last two, one each in Austria and Hungary, furnished the officers for the respective, national formation; Landwehr or Honved.

Initial gazetting of officers and their subsequent promotion was the prerogative of the Emperor who had the power to raise an officer to a rank for which he may not have had the necessary seniority. Promotion by seniority was the rule for ranks up to Major, by selection and by seniority up to Major General and entirely by selection above that rank. Promotion to field rank was conditional upon the Captain candidate having successfully completed a course at a Corps officers' school.

With the outbreak of war peacetime limitations to recruiting no longer applied. There was, of course, no transfer from active to reserve status and the minimum age at which a man was conscripted was reduced to 18. At the other end of the scale the maximum age to which he was required to serve was raised, firstly from 42 to 50 and then to 55. This latter move created unrest until the War Minister gave his assurance that men 50 and 55 would be used to perform only certain essential, but unarmed military duties. Men who had reached their 50th year were not automatically discharged from the Service but had to wait upon an Imperial decree which released them to go home on permanent leave.

In order to balance the constant drain of losses and to obtain the necessary recruits to man the battle line, medical standards were lowered, volunteers below the age of 18 were permitted to enlist, bodies of foreign troops like the Polish Legion were raised and wounded men, fresh from hospital, were drafted back to front line service. Only by such severe measures could the Armies of the Dual Monarchy be maintained at fighting strength.

2: The Infantry in general

THE news of the assassination, at Sarajevo, of the Archduke Franz Ferdinand and his consort, caused a wave of horror and indignation to sweep across the Empire. Many people, and not only those high in the Government or the military hierarchy, saw the complicity of Belgrade in the murders as a pretext to settle the Serbian question and the various diplomatic manoeuvrings together with the support of the German Government emboldened the Imperial authorities to bring the political situation to crisis point and to maintain it there.

It was, therefore, almost with a sense of relief from an unendurable tension that the orders announcing the various days of mobilisation were received and this feeling was general throughout the Empire, but nowhere felt more strongly than in the capital cities of Vienna and Budapest.

As a consequence of mobilisation and, almost overnight, it seemed, the shades of blue, the blacks and the golds of Infantry peacetime uniforms vanished from the fashionable boulevards to be replaced by a flood of pike-grey. The railway stations, the pavements, the very streets themselves were crowded with reservists, many of them marching as organised bodies, singing traditional and patriotic songs as they made their way to report to their Depots.

Inside many barracks there had been a complete breakdown in the system when more reservists poured in than could be dealt with and the men slept and ate when and where they could. Luckily the weather was clement so that those who had to sleep in the open were not too uncomfortable. But this chaos was not general and there were many regiments who not only absorbed their reservists, but were able to deal with the thousands of volunteers who came forward to serve their Sovereign. In the crowded barrack rooms and canteens the talk was of a short campaign to teach Serbia a lesson, for none thought of Austria as a large Empire threatening a small nation. Rather, most saw themselves as defenders of law and order, of the ideals represented by the city of Vienna—as upholders and defenders of Western culture, habits and morals against Slav barbarism.

In the first days, before the departure of fighting men had become commonplace and civilian participation lessened, the pattern of regiments departing on active service had been constant. On the day preceding departure a Field Mass was held and, upon this solemn occasion, the Regiment, once again, swore the oath of allegiance to the Monarch. The last hours were spent with families and friends until Tattoo at 9.30 pm called the soldiers back to the barracks from which they marched, in the heat of the following morning, to the railway station, accompanied by civilian cheers, the music of the bands and under a bombardment of flowers.

LEFT: *Men of a mountain unit moving up to the Front. The posy of flowers was the traditional gift to soldiers going out on active service.*

Four trains were needed to take each Regiment; the men in cattle trucks, the officers in carriages with the Regimental colour and the cash box in the Colonel's compartment. In the trucks the rank and file, probably already affected by the drink which had been pressed upon them, began to sing and to cheers, counter cheers and in a burst of patriotic fervour the Imperial armies of Habsburg, with three centuries of glory to sustain and to encourage them, set off to war. Not to the short campaign that they expected, but a world-wide conflict which was to shatter their regiments and which was to destroy utterly the Empire which they served.

What were they like these men of twleve or so different nations who served the Habsburg Emperors?

Most of them were peasants, accustomed from birth to early rising and to long hours of hard toil for a small wage. Their endurance was incredible and their demands small. Banded together in regiments they moved, during their period of service, from the Depot in which they received their basic training, to a battalion in some part of the vast Empire. In many cases the Regimental Depot was not in the regimental recruiting area. This was done to discourage desertion and to ensure that the loyalty of the soldiers was not undermined by fraternisation with civilians. The soldiers were, therefore, stationed among people whose language they did not speak. In their regiment, possible even in their battalion, would be men of other nations and the presence of these aliens acted as a spur to encourage the men to compete, militarily, against each other. Depots and garrison towns had little to offer in the way of entertainment except for the inn and, perhaps, a skittle alley. Not that the rank and file had much money to spend for the pay of an ordinary solider was 16 Heller a day (less than 1p) which, even by 1914 standards was quite low. There was a pay parade every tenth day. The scale of pay rose to £350 per annum for Colonels, via subaltern officers with the £85 per annum and Corporals on 1½p per day.

Pensions and other benefits were granted to long-service non-commissioned officers. Those with a minimum of twelve years' service had priority in State employment such as the Railway, the Customs or the Civil Service. Gratuities were given for more than 12 years' service and a State pension for 18 years or more. An officer retiring after 40 years' service received a pension equal to the salary he drew upon retirement.

It was an Army with a severe but fair discipline. Field punishment was to imprison a man in hand and ankle cuffs so that he could neither sit nor lie down and other confinements with handcuffs were normal sentence with hard labour. It was not until 1917 that both these punishments were discontinued. This is not to say that the Army was a brutal one. A Commission set up by the Socialists after the war investigated every alleged case of brutality by officers to their men and found none proven.

Like all armies of the period its fastest pace was that of the horse but mainly it was the Infantry's 100 paces to the minute, 24 minutes to the mile which regulated the marching columns. Despite the vast and efficient network of railways which covered the Empire, once outside the railway area then all movement was on foot. The normal day's march for small units was 12 miles (20 kms) and just under 9 miles (15 kms) for Corps or larger formations. The maximum length of a day's march was never to exceed 31 miles (50 kms) and this special effort could not be demanded for more than a few days in succession. This was not surprising for the soldiers carried most of their

LEFT: Field Service Marching Order, Spring, 1917. Note the blanket roll beneath the rucksack and the shoulder roll holding the rifle in position.

LEFT: Men of a Common Army infantry regiment being issued with rations. Note the way in which the haversack attaches to the waist belt.

equipment and clothing upon their backs. When fully laden the total weight carried by an Infantry soldier was 60 lb. The scale of clothing and equipment issued to the soldier going on active service was as follows:
1 cap; 1 jacket; 1 overcoat; 1 pair trousers; 1 pair gaiters or puttees; 1 shoulder roll; 2 sets of underclothing; 1 vest (cotton); 1 (ditto) pair pants; 1 neck cloth; 1 pair heavy and 1 pair light boots; 1 pair woollen gloves; 1 hide knapsack and 1 cartridge box with fittings; 1 Infantry style leather waist belt with buckle; 1 bayonet scabbard; 2 Infantry pattern leather cartridge pouches; 1 leather rifle sling; 2 overcoat straps; 2 pack straps; 1 haversack (known as a bread bag); 1 aluminium water bottle; identity document in a brass case, eating utensils, part of a tent and cleaning brushes.

Arms carried were normally the M95 magazine rifle, issued for all ranks from Corporal downwards, although in some cases the older rifle 88/90 was distributed, 1 bayonet. Each man carried 120 rounds of ammunition (40 of which were kept in the cartridge pouches, 80 in the cartridge box, under the knapsack). In every section there were 6 men equipped with a spade, two men with picks and one man with a wire cutter. Two pairs of flat pliers were also carried.

Marching Order was the double knapsack, cartridge pouches, water bottle, mess tin and cooking pot combined. The knapsack was of brown, undressed hide divided into two separate sections. The smaller, lower part contained 80 rounds of ammunition and a tinned soup ration. In the upper part was the greatcoat, emergency rations and clothing as well as part of the tent, three pegs and a section of the tent pole. The haversack (bread bag) contained the water bottle, knife and fork, bread ration and certain personal possessions.

The haversack was worn on the left side except for personnel (including drummers) who wore a sabre. Their haversack was then worn on the right.

ABOVE: Men of a Honved infantry regiment wearing Field Service Marching Order moving through a Polish village during the spring offensive of 1917. Note that some of the men do not have full equipment.

Some men were equipped with two haversacks. These were stretcher bearers, officers' servants, grooms and some bandsmen. Such personnel carried no ammunition pack. The Accounts Officer also carried a writing case in addition to his normal equipment.

On active service the complete ration consisted of $3\frac{1}{2}$ lb of bread or $2\frac{1}{4}$ lb of biscuit per day, 1 lb of meat (beef), $6\frac{1}{2}$ oz of vegetables and 2 issues of coffee. There was also, when possible, a daily issue of tobacco and 1 pint of wine. Bulk stores contained salt, pepper (paprika), fat, dried vegetables for soup, onion or garlic and vinegar. The normal ration differed from the full ration in the absence of onion, vinegar, wine and a reduction in the vegetable and the tobacco issue. There were also emergency rations.

Units were expected, on active service, to live off the country and to buy fresh meat on the hoof, which the Regimental cooks then slaughtered and prepared. With the Allied blockade the food situation within the Army deteriorated and the ration was continually cut. By September 1918 the ration strength of the Army in the Field was established as:

100,000 Officers and 2,568,000 Other Ranks on active service.

88,000 Officers and 1,256,000 Other Ranks, in the rear areas or in the homeland.

But even with these forces still available the Central Powers found themselves unable to continue the War and Austria-Hungary sued for peace. When it came

ABOVE: The Emperor Charles speaking to soldiers commended for bravery. The two men in the foreground are wearing variations on the standard Field Service Marching Order. The man immediately behind the officer is from an assault unit and carries a Repetierstutzen M95 rifle. He also has clipped to the side of his hat one of the badges illustrated on pages 68 and 69. The officer speaking to the Emperor has a cap patch showing his unit number. (IWM–Q64319).

the losses which the Empire had suffered were enormous.

From a total of 8,000,000 men who had seen service in the Army, Navy and Air Force, more than 1,016,000 had been killed, 1,691,000 men had been taken prisoner, although it must be remembered that this figure includes 12000 officers and 425,000 men who fell into the Allies hands at the time of the collapse, in November, 1918. More than 8000 officers and 470,000 men died as prisoners of war.

The losses among the Austro-German populations of Czechoslovakia (Moravia) were 44 per 1000 inhabitants; Carinthia 37; Bohemia 34; Salzburg, Tyrol, Steiermark and Vorarlberg 30-34, Oberösterreich 27 and Niederösterreich 22.

Among the non-German peoples the figure per thousand of the population was Czechoslovakia 22, Croats 20, Rumanians 23 and Italians 19. No figures for the Hungarian nation have been computed.

3: Infantry Organisation

'THE infantry is the main arm. Able to fight at long range or at close quarters, in defence and in attack, the infantry can use its weapons with success against any enemy, in every type of terrain, by day as well as by night. It decides battles: even without support from other arms and against a numerically superior enemy it is capable of attaining the laurels of victory, if only it has trust in itself and is imbued with the will to fight. For unyielding steadfastness combined with physical toughness qualify it to bring any battle, once begun, to a successful conclusion despite all obstacles and losses'.

Thus, paragraph one of the 1911 edition of the 'Exerzierreglement' clearly acknowledged the paramount role of the infantry within the Army organisation. The regiment was the basic formation of that arm not only in the Common Army but also in the Landwehr, the Honved and both Landsturm organisations.

Reducing the components of the Corps of Infantry to a simple thesis it may be stated that regiments or battalions were classifiable either as Heavy or Light and that the Light formations were the various types of Jäger found in the Imperial establishment. The subtle differences between the two types of infantry, as far as the British Army was concerned, had been gradually eliminated so that all regiments were part of the standard infantry organisation. But on the Continent, and particularly in Germany and Austria, Jäger formations were intended to carry out tactical tasks similar to those performed by Moore's Light Infantry in the Peninsula. Within the Austro-Hungarian establishment there were no special Guard regiments and the Jäger, particularly the four regiments of Kaiserjäger, were considered to be the élite of the Army.

One other unusual consideration marked the Imperial Force; its regiments although maintained from a Common Budget, were divided into German or Hungarian, depending upon the part of the Empire in which they had been raised. Under this arbitrary arrangement it was possible to find units composed of none other than Slavs or Italians and yet described as a German regiment. German, in this sense, meant that the regiment formed part of the German/Austro establishment of the Common Army.

Great emphasis was laid by the Imperial authorities on regional loyalty. All regiments, but particularly the Kaiserjäger and the Bosnians, were recruited from a specific province or recruiting area. Those regiments from whose sparsely populated counties an insufficient number of soldiers would have been recruited, were allowed to obtain their men from several districts of the Monarchy.

The previous section has shown that the 16 Army Corps districts were divided into 112 recruiting areas, three of which supplied the Fleet with men. Of the remaining 109 areas, one was allotted to each of the 102 regiments of the Common Army, three were retained for the four regiments of Kaiserjäger and one area each for the four regiments of Bosnian-Herzegovinian infantry. Within the establishment of the Common Army can also be included 32 battalions

ABOVE: Carts of an Austrian ration train in the Serbian campaign, 1914.

of Feldjäger, including one battalion of Bosnian Feldjäger and six companies of Bosnian Grenzjäger.

The Line regiments of the Common Army were numbered serially from 1 to 102. Both the Kaiserjäger and the Bosnian regiments were outside this numbering system and were listed I to IV, respectively.

Following normal military custom many Common Army regiments bore the name of a member of the Imperial dynasty or of a foreign Royal House who was their honorary Colonel. Preceding both the regimental name and number was an indication of the administration under which it served: Common Army regiments were described as 'Imperial and Royal' (kaiserlich. und königlich.), usually abbreviated to k.u.k. The full title of one such regiment, the 27th raised from Graz, capital city of the Archduchy of Styria, read 'The Imperial and Royal Infantry Regiment, Albert 1st, King of the Belgians, No 27'. The Kaiserjäger and the Bosnians had no such titling and were known by their regimental number.

The organisation of the Common Army regiments was based, both in peace time and for the greater part of the war, upon a system of four; that is, there were four battalions to a regiment (numbered I to IV) and each of these had four Companies (numbering from 1 to 16). In addition to the purely infantry companies each regiment fielded three machine-gun sections. A fourth section was raised for manoeuvres or in time of war. A Company was divided into four platoons, each of four sections.

The regimental administration was carried out from the Depot which housed the Reserve battalion cadre and was responsible for the forward movement of reinforcements, liaison and records. It was from the Depot that, in wartime, reinforcement formations known as 'Marsch' companies or battalions were assembled and despatched to join the regiment on active service. Each of these replacement units was numbered serially and, during the early years of the war, one battalion per month was sent to replace the wastage which the regiment suffered in the Line. By the middle of the war the manpower shortage reduced the supply of fresh troops and 'Marsch' formations were sent at longer intervals—usually every third month. Before a major offensive 'Marsch' battalions were grouped into Brigades and, in cases of extreme urgency, such as the need to reinforce, without delay, a regiment which had suffered severely, special 'Alarm' battalions were formed and despatched.

An infantry company's peacetime establishment was normally 99 officers and men but, under certan abnormal conditions, usually in frontier areas and only with the consent of the Minister of War, this number could be increased to 125. Under the usual establishment 85 non-commissioned officers and men had firearms. Stretcher bearers, officers' servants and other Company headquarters personnel had only sidearms. In an expanded Company the total armed was 112 of a strength of 125, all ranks. In war the strength of an average Company rose to 250 men and with 16 companies a regiment's fire power was 4041 rifles and eight machine-guns from a total of 4600 officers and men.

In 1914 the organisation of an infantry regiment was: Commander, Adjutant, Senior Medical Officer, Quartermaster, Chaplain, regimental trumpeter and two mounted orderlies. These, together with the Pioneer section of 1 officer and 72 men, constituted the regimental headquarters. There were four field companies in each of the four field battalions and a machine-gun section for each battalion. This was divided into two platoons each with a Schwarzlose machine-gun. The establishment of the machine-gun section was 1 officer and 25 men.

Each regiment or independent battalion was supplied by echelons of animals and carts. The battle train contained 32 mules or other animals carrying ammunition. Four other animals carried medical supplies. Each company had a cart, drawn by a pair of horses, in which was loaded rifle and machine-gun ammunition. Seventeen field kitchens, four armourers and a farrier completed the battle train. The pack mules each carried 2160 rounds of ammunition and in each company cart there was a further 9450 rounds. Thus the supply per rifleman was 120 rounds (which he carried on his person), 20 on the pack animals and 40 on the company cart. This vehicle also carried telephone equipment, pioneer tools, cobbler's equipment, a tailor's shop, maps, files and documents for the company office.

The supply train contained one repair waggon, 17 supply carts (one per company and one for regimental HQ), six supply mules for the machine-gun section and six baggage waggons. With this train travelled the unit Paymaster, the deputy supply officer and other auxiliaries.

A Jäger battalion contained a Headquarters, the Pioneer Platoon, four Companies each of four platoons, one machine-gun section and the two echelons, supply and battle.

BELOW: The Austrian Army made extensive use of dogs to pull small carts. Here animals are being used to tow infantry guns and light ammunition carts in Italy, 1917.

LEFT: The Austro-Hungarian Army also made use of dogs to locate wounded. Two animals of a regimental medical team are seen here with their handlers. The men are carrying the double haversack and the medical pouch which contained pain-killing drugs.

The mountain unit had no establishment for waggons or carts. All supplies and ammunition were brought up on pack animals. The battle train per battalion contained 28 ammunition mules, one ambulance, four telephone, six water, five food and one explosives animal.

The supply column had 22 animals laden with food boxes, four smithy mules, one for the mens' kit and four reserve animals.

Thus it can be seen that, at the outbreak of World War 1, the Army regiments and battalions comprised bodies of men armed only with rifles and machine-guns. These, then, depended upon the artillery, the sappers and the other ancillary arms to support and sustain them in the Line.

BELOW: Pack animals of an Austrian machine-gun section loaded with boxes of ammunition. (Italy, 1917).

Tactically, too, the Army was geared to fight the type of campaign which had obtained forty years before and this system of large masses, deploying slowly into lines with secure flanks, worked on the Eastern Front and against the Russians who were themselves tied to ponderous tactical manoeuvres. But with the entry of Italy into the war and the subsequent deployment of the bulk of the Imperial Army to defend the mountainous southern frontier, the Army underwent a series of crises.

In the isolated, remote and almost inacessible mountain areas the tactics and grouping which had been effective against the Russians, were useless, for a regiment could exercise only the loosest control over its effectives. The basic tactical formation ceased, therefore, to be the regiment and became instead the battalion and even reinforced companies.

Before World War 1, one battalion from each of 62 regiments had been detached for mountain warfare training, but even with this reserve of qualified Alpinists upon which to draw, the Austrian Army found itself in difficulties as units struggled to adapt themselves to the very different type of warfare that was fought in the Alpine snows.

To provide close support to infantry whose positions were so close to the enemy line that normal artillery would have been dangerous to use, pioneer sections were equipped, during 1915, with primitive mortars and as newer, more powerful types of trench artillery were introduced, these too were added to the regimental armoury. To this establishment was added the Infantry gun during 1916, the light machine-gun in 1917, flame-throwers and searchlights. The newer, more sophisticated weapons of modern warfare needed specially trained troops to use them to maximum effect and, to this end, a Technical Company was established in each regiment.

During 1917 a tactical reorganisation lowered regimental strengths to three thousand men and the number of platoons per company was reduced from four to three. The fourth platoon was then organised into two sections, each containing two light machine-guns. Early in 1918 a further reduction in establishments was introduced and regiments were organised on a three battalion

Regimental organisation

	Four battalion regiment	**1914**	
Regimental HQ	9 Officers	82 Other Ranks	(25 armed with rifles)
Battalion HQ	3 Officers	19 Other Ranks	(32 armed with rifles)
(This figure multiplied by four for the number of battalions)			
16 Companies	80 Officers	4192 Other Ranks	(3984 armed with rifles)
4 machine-gun sections	4 Officers	144 Other Ranks	(8 machine-guns)
	Three battalion regiment	**1917**	
Regimental HQ	11 Officers	82 Other Ranks	
Battalion HQ	4 Officers	14 Other Ranks	
(This figure multiplied by three for the number of battalions)			
3 battalions	60 Officers	1800 Other Ranks	
3 machine-gun Coys	15 Officers	480 Other Ranks	
12 light MG sections	12 Officers	300 Other Ranks	
Infantry gun section	1 Officer	24 Other Ranks	
Assault Company	3 Officers	150 Other Ranks	
Technical Company	3 Officers	120 Other Ranks	
	Independent battalion	**1917**	
Battalion HQ	8 Officers	36 Other Ranks	
4 Companies	20 Officers	600 Other Ranks	
MG Company	5 Officers	160 Other Ranks	
4 light MG Sections	4 Officers	140 Other Ranks	
Infantry Gun Section	1 Officer	25 Other Ranks	
Technical Section	3 Officers	94 Other Ranks	

basis. This move provided a large number of supernumary battalions and these were then formed into regiments. Forty new regiments were raised thereby and these were numbered serially from 102.

By 1918 the regiment was organised in the following manner: Commander, Headquarters platoon, Technical Company made up of several platoons including pioneers, searchlight, mortars and other special battle equipment together with a telephone platoon. Each of the three battalions had four Companies, three platoons of which were rifle and the fourth a light machine-gun platoon. Within each regiment there were four heavy machine-gun Companies each with eight machine-guns and two Infantry gun platoons each with two guns.

The assault platoon of each battalion was formed into a regimental Assault Company and the men of these well-trained storm troops, were excused guard duties and the more monotonous employments of trench life because of their dangerous and highly specialised abilities while in the Line. A Battle Train and Ration Column completed the establishment.

Thus, by the end of the war, the fire power of an average line Regiment of the Common Army had risen from just over 4000 rifles and eight machine-guns, to a point where it was a self-contained Command, having its own artillery, engineer detachments, assault troops and machine-gun Corps.

Regiments of the Common Army

The Imperial and Royal Infantry Regiment:	No
The Emperor	1
Alexander I, Tsar of Russia	2
The Archduke Charles	3
The Hoch und Deutschmeister	4
Freiherr von Klobucar	5
Charles I, King of Rumania	6
Count von Khevenhüller	7
The Archduke Charles Stephan	8
Count Elerfayt	9
Gustav V, King of Sweden	10
John George, Prince of Saxony	11
Parmann	12
Jung-Staremberg	13
Ernest Louis, Grand Duke of Hesse	14
Freiherr von Georgi	15
Freiherr von Giesl	16
Ritter von Milde	17
The Archduke Leopold Salvator	18
The Archduke Franz Ferdinand	19
Henry, Prince of Prussia	20
Count von Abensperg und Traun	21
Count von Lacy	22
Margrave von Baden	23
Ritter von Kummer	24
Edler von Pokorny	25
Schreiber	26
Albert I, King of the Belgians	27
Victor Emmanuel III, King of Italy	28
Freiherr von Loudon	29
Schoedler	30
Pucherna	31
The Empress and Queen Maria Theresa	32
The Emperor Leopold II	33
William I, German Emperor and King of Prussia	34
Freiherr von Sterneck	35
Reichsgraf Browne	36
The Archduke Josef	37
Alphonso XIII, King of Spain	38
Freiherr von Conrad	39
Ritter von Pino	40
The Archduke Eugene	41
Ernest Augustus, Duke of Brunswick	42
Rupert, Crown Prince of Bavaria	43

The Imperial and Royal Infantry Regiment:	No
The Archduke Albrecht	44
The Archduke Josef Ferdinand	45
(Vacant)	46
Count Beck-Rzikovski	47
Rohr	48
Freiherr von Hess	49
Frederick, Grand Duke of Baden	50
von Boroevic	51
The Archduke Frederick	52
Dankl	53
Alt-Starhemberg	54
Nicholas I, King of Montenegro	55
Count Daun	56
Prince of Sachsen-Coburg-Saalfeld	57
The Archduke Louis Salvator	58
The Archduke Rainer	59
Ritter von Ziegler	60
Ritter von Frank	61
Ludwig III, King of Bavaria	62
Freiherr von Pitreich	63
Ritter von Auffenberg	64
The Archduke Louis Victor	65
Peter Ferdinand	66
Freiherr Kray	67
Freiherr von Reicher	68
(Vacant)	69
Edler von Appel	70
Galgotszy	71
Freiherr von David	72
Albrecht, Duke of Württemberg	73
Freiherr von Schönaich	74
(Vacant)	75
Freiherr von Salis-Soglio	76
Philipp, Duke of Württemberg	77
Gerba	78
Graf Jellacic	79
Wilhelm Ernst, Grand Duke of Sachsen-Weimar-Eisenach	80
Freiherr von Walstätten	81
Freiherr von Schwitzer	82
Freiherr von Schikosky	83
Freiherr von Bolfras	84
von Gaudernak	85
Freiherr von Steininger	86
Freiherr von Succovaty	87
(Vacant)	88
Freiherr von Albori	89
Edler von Hosetzky	90
(Vacant)	91
Edler von Hootstein	92
(Vacant)	93
Freiherr von Koller	94
von Követz	95
Ferdinand, Crown Prince of Rumania	96
Freiherr von Waldstätten	97
von Rummer	98
(Vacant)	99
von Steinsberg	100
Freiherr von Drahtschmidt	101
Potiorek	102

Jäger and Bosnian Regiments

THE KAISERJÄGER

These four regiments had lower establishments than Common Army regiments and only the 2nd regiment had four battalions; the others had only three apiece.

The peacetime strength of such a regiment, excluding the Reserve battalion cadre, was 84 officers and 1570 men.

ABOVE: Bosnian troops heating coffee, Italy, 1917. Note the trouser leg button fastening and the fez exclusive to these troops.

The Kaiserjäger regiments had such a distinguished career during the Great War that on January 16, 1917, the Emperor bestowed upon the 8th Infantry Division the distinction of 'Kaiserjäger' Division in recognition of the conspicuous gallantry with which it had fought on both the eastern and the southern fronts.

THE BOSNIAN-HERZEGOVINIAN INFANTRY REGIMENTS

Like the Kaiserjäger, the Bosnian units of the Monarchy were considered to be élite formations and had four regiments on the peacetime establishment.

Each had its full complement of four battalions and in some cases, supernumary battalions were raised which were converted into Feldjäger battalions, except in one case when a fifth regiment was formed during the war, from the supernumaries.

When the reduction to three battalion regiments was ordered, the units released thereby were combined to form a further three regiments.

Other troops raised from Bosnia were thirteen Lines-of-communication battalions.

FELDJÄGER BATTALIONS

Whereas the Kaiserjäger and the Bosnian regiments had drawn their men from certain defined areas of the Monarchy, the soldiers of the Feldjäger battalions had been recruited from the mountainous areas of the whole Empire. The Feldjäger were intended to form a light and mobile extension of the élite Kaiserjäger and, in fact, Feldjäger battalions 3, 15 and 26 were incorporated into the Kaiserjäger establishment as ordinary battalions of those regiments.

ORDER OF BATTLE OF A FELDJÄGER BATTALION
AUGUST 1914

AUGUST 1918

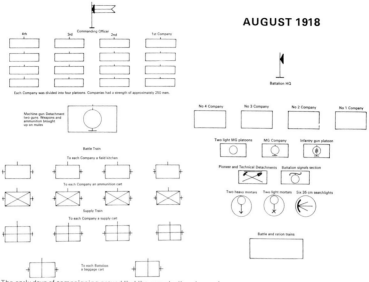

The early days of campaigning proved that the organisation shown above was unwieldy and to the battle train was added 1 tools and equipment cart and a medical cart. The supply train was increased by two baggage waggons so that each Company had one. A cart acting as a mobile smithy was added to the train. Where required carts were requisitioned from local sources.

The pre-war establishment allowed for 32 battalions, one of which had been raised from Bosnia. During the war the total of Feldjäger battalions was raised to 42, of which eight were Bosnian and one was a composite battalion made up of the cyclist companies from four battalions.

The 1914 establishment of a Feldjäger battalion was normally four Companies but Nos 11, 20, 24 and 29 battalions had only three field companies each and a machine-gun section. The No 4 company of each of these four battalions was mounted on collapsible bicycles. Cyclist companies were made up of three platoons and a machine-gun platoon. They also had two lorries, two motor cycles and a cyclist first-aid detachment on strength.

Independent rifle battalions had a peacetime strength of 24 officers and 395 other ranks exclusive of the Reserve Company cadre.

GRENZJÄGER BATTALIONS

These all originated in the six companies of Grenzjäger raised in Bosnia-Herzegovina. Their peacetime establishment was by platoons and the number per Company varied from between three and five. Their function was frontier control but, when in 1916, each Company was expanded to battalion strength, they were sent on active service to Albania.

HIGHER COMMANDS

The peacetime organisation of the army did not allow for combinations greater than a Corps, of which there were sixteen, corresponding to the military districts shown on the map on page 14.

ORDER OF BATTLE OF AN INFANTRY DIVISION AS AT:

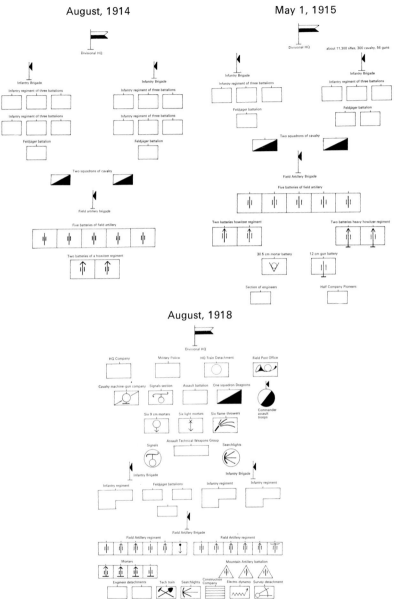

In addition to the above there were local artillery and technical troops and various types of train.

Even before the war the composition of a Corps was by no means a rigidly determined one, although the ideal balance striven for was two Common Army divisions to one Landwehr. To achieve this there were 49 divisions on the peacetime establishment; 33 of them Common Army, eight Landwehr and eight Honvéd. (see table).

By the end of the war 71 divisions and 14 independent Brigades had been raised, as a result of this expansion, the number of Corps was increased to 26.

These Corps were formed into nine Armies: 1–7, 10 and 11, and were disposed on the three, major theatres of operations. These were Eastern, Balkan and South Western (Italy). It is noteworthy that only the Italian Front had an Austrian as Commander-in-Chief.

Peacetime establishment of divisions

Common Army divisions: 1 – 12, 14 – 19, 24, 25, 27 – 36, 47, 48. (No 49 was broken up at the outbreak of the war).
Landwehr: 13, 21, 22, 26, 43 – 46.
Honved: 20, 23, 37 – 42.

ESTABLISHMENTS

Within the Imperial Army there were two establishments; Normal and Mountain.

With the normal establishment we have already dealt and the difference between that and the organisation of a mountain unit was:

The transport for the formation was carried entirely by pack animal. The weight of ammunition and the scale of equipment was reduced. There was no divisional ammunition column but every second battalion of infantry had a mountain artillery column containing 1 officer and 70 other ranks. Tactically, there was a greater freedom of action for small units, and numbers within the unit were higher than in normal Common Army companies, battalions and regiments.

As the Imperial Army had raised certain regiments as mountain troops and had detached other battalions from Common Army regiments for mountain training, it follows, therefore, that certain divisions were, specifically, mountain divisions. These were: Nos 1, 18, 47, 50, 57–60, 72 and 89.

BELOW: A stone built defensive position on the Italian Front, 1916, manned by men of an infantry unit and a dismounted cavalry regiment. Note the boots, heavily studded in the Infantry fashion.

2nd Lieutenant, Common Army Infantry Regiment No 45. Parade Dress

Private Soldier, Common Army Infantry Regiment No 64. Parade Dress

4: Landwehr organisation

WHEN, in 1867, the Austrian authorities conceded to the Hungarians the right to raise and maintain their own territorial military force independent of the Imperial government, the army which was to be raised in Hungary needed to be balanced by a similar organisation covering the Austrian provinces. Thus there came into existence the Austrian Landwehr and the Hungarian Honved.

The original intention had been to implement the plan formulated by the Archduke Charles for a second line army of trained men, garrisoned in and able to defend their native provinces but, given the fact of the manpower shortage in the Army, this was an intention with no hope of realisation.

It is, therefore, incorrect to consider either the Landwehr or the Honved as territorial forces in the sense of the British Army's use of that term: that is of a force of part-time soldiers, for the men of these Austro-Hungarian formations underwent full time military training during the whole of their service with the colours. In one respect indeed, that of mountain training, the Landwehr was able to furnish an élite corps unequalled by any other similar force in the world.

THE AUSTRIAN LANDWEHR

The Austrian Landwehr organisation paralleled that of the Common Army and divided Austria into nine districts. From each of eight of these a Landwehr Division could be raised: from the ninth area, Ragusa, only two regiments were obtained. During the latter part of the World War a ninth Landwehr Division was raised.

As the money for the Landwehr was voted by the Austrian 'Delegation' and, therefore, its administration came within the province of the Austrian Defence Ministry, the Force was classified as Imperial Royal (kaiserlich. königlich).

As early as 1869 cadres had been formed around which companies and, later battalions were raised and these were combined regimentally, by 1901. With the raising of the Landsturm in 1887, for territorial defence, the Landwehr ceased officially, to be considered as a militia having neither artillery nor technical troops, but became instead an Army in organisation, in equipment and in weapons. Austrian Landwehr regiments formed Brigades and Divisions and followed Common Army regimental practice, in the years between 1908 and 1912, of forming a machine-gun section for each battalion of the regiment.

ABOVE: Men of an Infantry gun section of a Landwehr Infantry regiment, Eastern Front, 1917. Note the telescopic sight on the gun and the unofficial badges on the nearest man's cap.

The Force contained 37 regiments, numbered in sequence, but No 4 and No 27 were detached for service with the Landwehr mountain troops. All regiments were titled from the district in which they had been raised and bore that name, together with their number and their administrative description. Thus the 21st Regiment was titled 'The Imperial Royal Landwehr Infantry Regiment St Pölten, No 21'.

One unusual feature of the Austrian Landwehr was that its regiments bore neither colours nor had regimental bands, although music could be provided by grouping the regimental trumpeters and buglers under a bandmaster. In 1917 the Emperor-King Charles, acting upon the advice of von Georgi, the Austrian Defence Minister, was pleased to rename all units as Schützen instead of the term Landwehr, as a mark of his recognition of the valour with which they had conducted themselves during the war.

Although the usual establishment was for a three battalion regiment with four companies to a battalion, these numbers could be increased or reduced. This was the case in the specialist, mountain warfare formations of whom the Landwehr fielded two types: the Landesschützen (renamed as Kaiserschützen in 1917) and the Landwehr infantry regiments Nos 4 and 27 who were renamed Gebirgsschützen regiments No 1 and 2, in the same year.

The three regiments of Kaiserschützen had the following establishments: four, three and four battalions with thirteen, nine and ten Companies respectively. The 1st, Gebirgsschützen regiment had a full complement of three battalions but, until the latter stages of the war, the 2nd regiment had only two battalions. The three battalions of the 1st regiment produced ten companies while the 2nd, regiment's battalions made up nine companies.

The peacetime strength of the Landwehr infantry companies was lower than that of the Common Army companies except in the case of the Landwehr mountain troops. Their company strengths were, in peacetime, up to twenty men larger than in the normal Common Army company. During the war the strength of the ordinary Landwehr companies was raised so that by 1917, their establishments and those of the Common Army were the same.

2nd Lieutenant, Common Army Infantry Regiment No 99. Walking-Out Dress with greatcoat.

Lieutenant, Common Army Infantry Regiment No 41. Walking-Out Dress.

Major, Kaiserjäger Regiment. Parade Dress.

Bosrian - Herzegovinian Private Soldier, Common Army Infantry Regiment. Parade Dress.

The larger establishment in Mountain Companies was maintained and, in the specially raised Alpine Companies (Hochgebirgskompanien), was increased so that their numbers were in excess of the Line infantry. Each of these Alpine Companies contained three platoons, one heavy machine-gun section of two guns, four guide sections, two telephone sections and a technical section.

Alpine Companies acted as guides to troops who were fighting in the mountains and by use of special Alpine skills, enabled the troops to overcome the difficulties of terrain. When acting as guides the tactical unit employed was usually the Section, but platoons and even Companies were frequently used as Assault troops during battles in the snows of the high Alps.

In addition to the normal arms and equipment the Alpinists were issued with ice picks, climbing ropes, climbing boots and, where necessary, ski-ing equipment. At least twenty such Companies were raised and they were numbered to conform with the number of the Brigade or Division to which they had originally been attached. Because of their detachment to, and employment by, other formations this numbering eventually ceased to have any significance as a form of identification.

Regiments of the Austrian Landwehr as at August, 1914

The Imperial Royal Landwehr Infantry Regiment:

	No
Vienna	1
Linz	2
Graz	3
Klagenfurt	4

RIGHT: Men of a Kaiserschützen unit in Bolzano, 1917. The soldiers are wearing Field Service Marching Order of the old pattern. The rifle is the Gewehr M 95.

The Imperial Royal Landwehr Infantry Regiment:	No
Pola	5
Eger (Bohemia)	6
Pilsen	7
Prague	8
Leitmeritz	9
Jungbunzlau	10
Jicin	11
Caslau	12
Olmütz	13
Brünn	14
Troppau	15
Cracow	16
Rzeszov	17
Przemysl	18
Lvov	19
Stanislav	20
St Pölten	21
Czernovitz	22
Zara	23
Vienna	24
Kremsier	25
Marburg	26
Laibach	27
Pisek	28
Budejovice	29
Hohenmauth	30
Teschen	31
Neusandez	32
Stryj	33
Jaroslav	34
Zloczow	35
Kolomea	36
Gravosa	37

Landesschützen Regiments

Nos I
 II
 III

Landwehr and Landesschützen regiments changed their names to Schützen and Kaiserschützen respectively.

RIGHT: This highly decorated soldier is a mountain guide wearing the rope and other specialised equipment of his unit. He wears three silver medals for bravery and a wound cross.

Major, Common Army Infantry Regiment No 35. Field Service Dress with greatcoat.

Private Soldier, Common Army Infantry Regiment No 41. Field Service Dress with greatcoat

Private Soldier, Kaiserschützen Regiment. Field service Dress 1914.

Private Soldier, Royal Hungarian Landwehr (Honved). Field Service Dress.

LANDWEHR INFANTRY DIVISIONS

The 13th Landwehr, or Schützen Division fought on the Eastern Front until July 1917 when it was transferred to Rumania. In September of that year it was posted to Italy where it remained until the end of the war.

The 21st Division fought in Poland until June 1917 when it went to Italy. In November 1917 it was transferred to the Tyrol where it remained until the spring of 1918 when it came back to the Italian theatre of operations.

The 22nd, was in Poland until November 1915 when it left the Eastern Front for Italy. Like the 21st, it was posted to the Tyrol until 1916 when it came back to the Italian Front.

The 26th, was on the Eastern Front until February 1918 when it was transferred to Italy.

The 43rd, was in Poland until March 1916 when it was posted, first to the Tyrol and then to Italy. It returned to Russia in November 1917. After frontier duties in the Mogilev area it returned to Italy for the third battle along the Piave river in October 1918.

The 44th Division was in Poland until June 1915 when it was transferred to Italy. From Italy it went to Carinthia and from thence to the Tyrol in 1916. It became an instructional unit in the spring of 1918 and returned to active service for the Piave battles. The division was captured on November 4, 1918.

The 45th Division was in Poland until March 1918 and was then transferred to Bosnia. The 46th, was also on the Eastern Front until spring 1918 when it was posted to Italy.

The 54th, was raised from the former 54th Infantry Division, in February 1916. It fought on the Eastern Front and was in the Army of Occupation in the Ukraine from January to May 1918. It then evacuated the area at the end of October 1918.

The 56th Division was raised from the Adige Valley Group at the beginning of October 1917. It first saw action as a Landwehr Division in the Adige in the spring of 1918 and was captured near Trient on November 4, 1918.

The nine Area Commands of the Austrian Landwehr Administration

Headquarters	Area covered	Formed
Cracow	West Galicia, Silesia and northern Moravia	46th Landwehr Division
Vienna	Lower Austria and southern Moravia	13th Landwehr Division
Graz	Styria, Carinthia, Trieste, Carniola, Istria, Gorizia and Gradisca	22nd Landwehr Division
Prague	South western Bohemia	21st Landwehr Division
Leitmeritz	North eastern Bohemia	26th Landwehr Division
Przemysl	Central Galicia	45th Landwehr Division
Lemberg	East Galicia and Bukovina	43rd Landwehr Division
Innsbruck	Tyrol, Vorarlberg, Upper Austria and Salzburg	44th Landwehr Division
Ragusa	Dalmatia	23rd and 37th, Landwehr Regiments.

(NB, Landwehr divisions and regiments changed their titles to Schützen divisions and regiments during 1917).

ABOVE: This posed picture is of an Austrian Landsturm unit defending a village in Poland. Note the Infantry sabre M62 and the M 88/90 pattern rifles.

THE AUSTRIAN LANDSTURM

Like the Landwehr the Landsturm came under the administration of the Austrian Defence Minister and the formations of this organisation were also entitled 'Imperial Royal'.

The concept of a levee en-masse, which is essentially what the Landsturm represented was not a new idea, but the role which the Force was intended to play upon its resurrection in 1887, certainly was. It was to be a militarily potent force forming the second line of Austria's Army and, to fulfil this role, was to be shaped along the lines of the Common Army and Landwehr organisations.

However, there was in peacetime, no regimental establishment and it was only during the war that nineteen Landsturm regiments were raised. (Provisional cadres had been set up for a proposed total of seventeen regiments. A further two regiments were raised during the war). Their regimental number agreed with that of the Landsturm Command in which the regiment had been raised. The Austrian establishment formed only infantry units, but both infantry and cavalry formations were produced from the Hungarian Landsturm organisation.

Acting in the role of defenders of their native provinces it is no surprise, therefore, to note that the Landsturm units fought in battles on the Eastern Front and that, as a result of their ability, an increasing use was made of them in active military operations. But however keenly the Landsturm soldier may have been resolved to fight for his native province, it is true to say that he was severely handicapped by the low priority which his force had, vis-a-vis the Common Army or the Landwehr, in the question of supplies and arms. In many cases Landsturm units went into action in antique uniforms—sometimes with only an armband on their civilian clothes to indicate that they were soldiers—and with rifles that had been declared obsolete years earlier.

By September 1918, a total of fifteen Landsturm regiments was still in the line, together with a large number of independent battalions on line-of-communication, guard and other rear area duties. It was, usually only in these independent battalions, that the proposed establishment of four companies to a battalion was reached.

2nd Lieutenant, Royal Hungarian Landwehr (Honved). Parade Dress.

2nd Lieutenant, Common Army Infantry Regiment No 13. Field Service Dress, 1914.

2nd Lieutenant, Common Army Infantry Regiment No 41. Field Service Dress, 1918.

Private Soldier, Common Army Infantry Regiment No 13. Field Service Dress and Equipment

RIGHT: This Soldier of a Standschützen unit wears the pre-1907 uniform with shoulder wings in regimental colour. Note also the various medals he wears. They include the silver and gold medals for bravery won in 1849 and 1866 respectively.

STANDSCHÜTZEN UNITS

The origins of these formations went back to the early seventeenth century when rifle clubs were formed in Tyrol and in Vorarlberg for sporting purposes. Because of the intense loyalty of the people of Tirol to the Emperor, particularly during the Napoleonic invasion, the Habsburg monarchs gave to the men of those regions the right to bear arms 'in perpetuo'. By the late nineteenth century the Standschützen organisation had become firmly established and among the privileges peculiar to the force was the right to elect its own officers and non-commissioned officers, although it was usual for the establishment to include a regular Army adviser on tactics.

War mobilisation of the able-bodied members left the clubs with only men too old or boys too young for active service, but when Italy entered the war, true to tradition, the clubs offered to form local defence companies. This offer was accepted and they were then absorbed into the Army organisation. Each club supplied a platoon, the platoons of a particular area formed a company and the companies from a district made up a battalion. Each battalion was named after the locality in which it had been raised; South Tyrol, alone, raised forty battalions.

As the organisation was primarily a civilian one the Standschützen did not bear properly presented, official colours, but many districts had flags made which were then carried by the local unit. Most of these flags were laid up when the battalion marched out to war.

Shortages in uniform and equipment, together with the peculiar administration of the Standschützen was responsible for many of the unusual features connected with this organisation. Rations were usually cooked by local villagers and brought up to the men by members of their own families. One woman, Viktoria Says, lost a leg on Whitsunday 1917, while acting as food carrier for her father. In the early days of the war men went into action carrying their own rifles and dressed in civilian clothes. To meet the conditions of the

Geneva Convention regarding uniform a black/gold armband was worn. When uniform was issued a green/white armband worn on the left arm denoted that the wearer was Standschützen. The trousers were the usual mountaineering pattern and with them thick socks were worn instead of puttees. Rank devices worn on the jacket consisted of rosettes instead of stars, and the collar bore either the eagle of Tirol or the arms of Vorarlberg to denote the battalion's territorial loyalty. Standschützen units wore neither an Edelweiss badge nor the black cock feather bush in their caps.

Officer's sword knots, originally silver embossed with the eagle of Tirol, were changed to gold in recognition of the bravery of Standschützen units.

Early in the war the loyalty of the force was put to a severe and unnecessary test. In an attempt to prevent Italy declaring war upon her, Austria offered to cede some of her territory in South Tyrol. The storm which this news created in all the Tyrolean regiments, but particularly among the Standschützen from that area, caused the authorities to doubt the reliability of the battalions but, when Italy entered the war the allegiance to Habsburg was no longer in doubt.

The Standschützen organisation raised 75 battalions for Austria but the high casualty rate which they suffered reduced many to company strength. These units were then either amalgamated with other understrength battalions or, in some cases, disbanded altogether.

By the middle of 1918 there were only ten groups of Standschützen in the field, numbering some 30 battalions.

VOLUNTEER RIFLE BATTALIONS

The outbreak of war produced many patriotic gestures from the German peoples of the Empire and one of these was the formation of rifle units, which paralleled the Standschützen organisation of Tyrol and Vorarlberg, in other provinces of Austria proper.

A total of nine battalions of volunteers was raised; three from Carinthia, the others from Salzburg, Styria, Lower Austria and Upper Austria. By the end of the war the six battalions from the other provinces were still in the Field but only one of the Carinthian battalions was still on active service.

THE POLISH LEGION

The chief organiser of the Legion which fought for Austria was Josef Pilsudski, later to become President of an independent Poland.

He had organised rifle clubs along the lines of the Standschützen organisation, and secretly mobilised his men on August 2, 1914. During the night of August 6, Pilsudski led elements of his League of Riflemen into Galicia. The invading force was only 172 men strong, organised into three Companies, and the assault was made without the approval of the Austrian authorities. By the middle of August the Legion was officially declared to be part of the Austrian Landwehr and was given certain privileges which included the right to wear distinctive badges, to have Polish officers and to use Polish instead of German as the language of command.

The uniform of the Legion was basically that of the Austrian Army, with national distinctions. Piping and patches were normally red, buttons were white metal. Rank badges followed the Austrian pattern and consisted of white and silver stars. The white eagle of Poland, in woven cloth or in metal, decorated the head-dress.

Yellow Infantry Colour (Eagle on both sides)

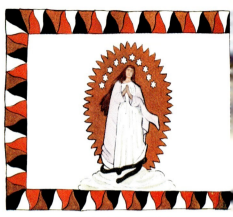
White Infantry Colour (Eagle on reverse)

Badges of Rank

Gefreiter
(Lance Corporal)

Korporal or Unterjäger
(Corporal)

Zugsfuhrer
(Sergeant)

Feldwebel/Wachtmister
Oberjäger
(Sergeant-Major)

Stabsunteroffizier

Offizierstellvertreter

Leutnant
(2nd Lieutenant)

Oberleutnant
(Lieutenant)

Hauptmann
(Captain)

Major

Oberstleutnant
(Lieutenant-Colonel)

Oberst
(Colonel)

General-Major
(Major-General)

Feldmarschalleutnant
(Lieutenant-General)

General d. Inf
(General)

General-Oberst
(Colonel-General)

Feldmarschall
(Field-Marshal)

RIGHT: Officers of the Polish Legion at a ceremony in Warsaw. Note the distinctive collar piping and the Polish eagle cap badge. The officer on the left wears the ribbon of the German Iron Cross in his buttonhole.

One completely distinctive decoration, identifying the battalions which wore it as unmistakably Polish, was the zig-zag lines of piping roung the collar. These were coloured red or white and were either in metal or wool. Many Legionaires wore the distinctive soft cap with a Prussian peak and the men of the 1st Brigade wore a tunic with exposed buttons. The other Brigades conformed more closely to the usual Austrian cap and jacket tunic with concealed buttons.

By October 1914 the Legion had sufficient recruits to organise six infantry battalions, a cavalry squadron and some artillery. With the capture of parts of the Russian Empire, large numbers of men flocked to the recruiting centres which had been opened in the main cities of Poland. The numbers enlisted enabled the Legion to expand to a strength of seven infantry regiments (numbered from one to seven) each with the usual Landwehr establishment of three battalions. From these seven regiments a force of three infantry brigades was formed, two of which were supported by a regiment of Uhlans (each of six squadrons), a Polish artillery regiment and a Pioneer detachment. A third Brigade was infantry without supporting arms or cavalry.

The prowess of the Polish Legion encouraged the central powers to consider the declaration of a completely independent Poland and the raising of a future Polish Army. The Austrian Emperor. recognising that such a Poland would be within the German sphere of influence, passed the Legion and its administration over to the German Governor-General. This move angered the Poles and many who protested were interned or imprisoned.

The Legion itself was disbanded and the Poles who had been members of the Austro/Polish regiments of the Habsburg Army were either returned to their Depots or drafted to other units. The 2nd Polish Brigade remained loyal to Austria-Hungary until the news was received that part of Poland had been ceded to the Ukrainian Government which had been formed after the Russian revolution. The whole Brigade then went over, en masse, to the Soviet Army.

THE UKRAINIAN LEGION

This formation was based upon the larger and more successful Polish Legion and was formed of Ruthenians from Galicia, to fight against Russia. A regiment of two battalions was formed and suffered such severe casualties during the summer campaign of 1916 that it was withdrawn from the Front. In 1918 a battalion of the Legion was serving with an independent Landsturm Brigade in Bessarabia.

The survivors of the regiment which had had such severe losses during 1916 were formed into a cadre around which the Army of the independent State of the Ukraine was formed after the Russian revolution.

ABOVE: Volunteers for the Albanian Legion marching to the recruiting depot accompanied by a tribal flag. Note the white pants with coloured braiding.

THE ALBANIAN LEGION

The Habsburg authorities set to work, during 1916, to organise a regular Albanian militia conscripted on a territorial basis, only excepting from this compulsory service the irregular tribal bands of northern Albania which had been placed voluntarily at the disposal of the Austrian occupation forces.

The total strength of this force was nine battalions, each of four companies. Company strength was normally between 150 to 175 men. Officers and senior non-commissioned officers were Austro-Hungarian.

The battalions were armed with captured rifles but each had a company armed with the Austrian Schwarzlose machine-gun.

The basic uniform of the Austrian infantry was worn and the cap bore a cockade in black and red, the national colours of Albania. Officers' uniforms were further distinguished by black and red piping on the collar.

ASSAULT TROOPS

It was not until the end of 1916 that the Austrian authorities recognised that the unofficial assault formations which had been formed should become an integral part of the military organisation and they, therefore, regularised these units by establishing a storm troop hierarchy.

This is not to say that there was a rigid establishment, although, as a general rule, a platoon was raised from each battalion of a regiment and combined with other platoons to form an assault battalion. The tactical employment of this battalion was decided by the Division who could allot extra troops or additional equipment to support a particular operation, but platoons usually served with their battalions, unless grouped for certain missions.

The role of the storm troops was to undertake fighting patrols and during the opening attacks of an offensive, to penetrate the enemy's trench system or neutralise his strong points. To enable the men to achieve these tasks the training which was given was both arduous and thorough and the scale of equipment to support them was lavish. Tactically a battalion assault would be spearheaded by patrols in platoon strength, lightly equipped but carrying a high proportion of grenades and pistols. Once the patrols had broken the enemy trench line they would form a bridgehead by extending along the trenches, destroying opposition wherever it was encountered. Supporting the storm platoons were detachments of assault pioneers, trench mortar and light machine-gun teams. Accompanying this second wave were the medical sections and telephone group—all of whom were, themselves, assault trained. To reinforce an attack the storm troops could call upon infantry gun, mountain

RIGHT: A sergeant from a storm unit on guard near Vertojba (Isonzo Front), August, 1917. He is wearing an Austrian pattern steel helmet, gas mask, trench dagger and bomb bags. His rifle is the Repetiergewehr M95 and the bayonet is fitted with the decorative although functional knot.
(IWM-Q64324).

artillery support or, where necessary, portable flame throwers. Once the assault had succeeded the storm troops were then relieved by regular infantry who followed close behind them.

The storm troop uniform was the infantry tunic and trousers, frequently distinguished by reinforcement patches at the knee and elbow, puttees and boots. Steel helmets and gas masks were always carried. In addition each man carried a rucksack, a portering frame, two sacks for hand grenades, four sandbags, a torch, pick or shovel, a double issue of emergency rations and two water bottles.

Arms carried were pistols or carbines, a dagger, two sorts of hand grenades and a higher than normal issue of flare pistols, signalling flags, lamps and wire cutters. During the last year of the war an increasing use was made of the linked barrel, 9 mm assault machine pistols.

The successes achieved by storm troops was such that the Army authorities proposed training the whole infantry arm in the same tactics. This proposal never materialised.

BELOW: An Assault Company of storm troops forming up for an attack along the Isonzo river, 1917. The large plate over the shoulder of the nearest man is the base plate for a light mortar. The last man just visible on the left is carrying ammunition for this in his portering frame.

5: Honved organisation

THIS force was raised as a result of Hungarian demands for a national, Magyar-speaking Army and the name Honved (Defender of the Country) was included in the Hungarian title of every unit.

As the Honved regiments were paid for out of the Hungarian Estimates voted by the Magyar 'Delegation' and were, therefore, under the administration of the Hungarian Minister of Defence, they were titled 'Royal Hungarian' (königlich. ungarisch.). Conforming to Austrian procedure they were named from the district in which they had been raised and bore that name as well as as their regimental number ie, 'The Royal Hungarian Sopron Landwehr Infantry Regiment, No 18'.

Unlike the Austrian Landwehr the Honved carried colours and had bands, although these were not regimentally organised. The force mustered seven bands one of which was stationed in each of the six districts into which the Honved organisation was divided. The seventh band was stationed in the garrison town of the 20th Honved Infantry Division in Nagyvarad.

The establishing of a national Army was greeted with great enthusiasm by the Magyar nation and recruits were obtained from the six Army Corps districts, which paralleled the Common Army areas. Soon Companies with an average strength of 55 men each were formed. Then followed a series of amalgamations into 82 battalions, of whom four were Croat, and these 82 battalions were formed into four battalion regiments during 1890.

The 1912 reorganisation reduced the regimental establishment to three battalions (the one exception was the 19th Regiment which had four; the fourth coming from Fiume). Several battalions were under strength and eleven of them had only three companies. The battalions surplus to establishment under the reorganisation were themselves formed into regiments and when this had all been completed the Honved force consisted of 32 regiments, numbered in sequence. Provision had been made for one machine-gun section per battalion but this had not been achieved at the outbreak of the Great War.

It was not until 1913 that the Imperial authorities granted the right to include artillery in the Honved establishment so that it was no longer a purely infantry and cavalry organisation dependent upon the Common Army for artillery and ancillary services. By this move it was demonstrated that the original intention of raising the Honved as a purely territorial force had had to be abandoned and that it would take its place in the fighting line with the regular Army, wherever it was called to serve.

The losses which the Honved Army suffered during the Great War required that new regiments be recruited. By the end of 1914 a further five had been formed, over and above the peacetime number, and during the subsequent years others were raised so that a total of 47 regiments were on active service. The numbering sequence of these newly raised regiments did not follow directly on but began with 300 and finished with 316. In September 1918 there were 44 regiments in the line.

Honved Infantry Regiments as at August, 1914

The Royal Hungarian Landwehr Infantry Regiment:	No
Budapest	1
Gyula	2
Debrezin	3
Nagyvarad	4
Szegedin	5
Szabadka	6
Versecz	7
Lugos	8
Kassa	9
Miskolcz	10
Munkacs	11
Szatmar-Nemeti	12
Poszony	13
Nyitra	14
Trencsen	15
Beszterczebanya	16
Szekesferjervar	17
Sopron	18
Pecs	19
Nagykaniza	20
Kolozsvar	21
Maros-Vasarhely	22
Nagyszeben	23
Brasso	24
Zagreb	25
Karlovac	26
Sisak	27
Osijek	28
Budapest	29
Budapest	30
Veszprem	31
Des	32

Upon mobilisation in 1914 eight divisions of Honved infantry were put into the Field. The 20th Division, intended for Serbia was sent to the Eastern Front was then deployed to Italy, returned to Russia and was then posted back to Italy where it served until the end of the war.

The 23rd Division was also intended for Serbia but went instead to defend Przemysl. During the siege of this town it was completely destroyed. It was reported that the Division lost 68 per cent of its strength during three days of fighting.

The 37th Division, having served against the Russians was sent, in 1916, to Rumania and from there to Italy during 1918. It was then sent to France, the only Honved Division to serve in that theatre of operations but it arrived too late to take part in the fighting.

The 38th Division was on the Eastern Front until the end of 1917 when it was deployed to Italy and was decimated during the battles of February, 1918.

The 39th Division fought on the Russian Front until 1916 when it was transferred to the Rumainian theatre of operations. It was then sent back to Hungary in March 1918 and returned to active service at the end of July 1918. From July until November 1918 it served on the Italian Front.

The 40th Division served in Serbia until it was posted to the Carpathian Front during 1915. There it served until March 1918 when it went, firstly to Croatia, and finally to Italy in July of that year.

The 41st Division served on the Eastern Front until the end of 1916 and was then transferred to Italy where it served until the end of the war.

The 42nd Division was a Croatian Division and fought against Serbia. It was then sent to serve in the Carpathians, then in the Army of Occupation in the Ukraine and, finally to Italy.

The 51st Division was raised during 1915 and saw service in Poland until August 1916 when it was transferred from Poland to Italy where it served until the end of the war.

The 64th, was raised during October 1917 and served for the whole of its service on the Italian Front.

The 70th, raised during October 1915, served on the Russian Front until its transfer to the Rumainian theatre during 1917. In January 1918 it left the Balkan theatre for the Italian Front.

The 74th, was raised during April 1917 for service in Rumania. During May 1918 it was transferred to Italy.

The 155th, (formerly the 55th Infantry Division) was re-constituted during October 1917 and served in the Ukraine until May 1918 when it was posted to the Rumanian theatre of operations.

The six Area Commands of the Hungarian Honved organisation

No	Headquarters	Area covered	Formed
I	Budapest	Central Hungary	40th and 41st Honved Divisions
II	Szeged	Southern Hungary	23rd Honved Division
III	Kassa	Northern Hungary	39th Honved Division
IV	Pozsony	Western Hungary	37th Honved Division
V	Koloszvar	Transylvania	38th Honved Division
VI	Agram (Zagreb)	Croatia and Slavonia	42nd Honved Division

These Command Areas are applicable for the recruiting of the Hungarian Landsturm organisation.
The 20th Honved Division was raised from the II, III and Vth Honved Area Commands.

THE HUNGARIAN LANDSTURM

As this force came within the administration of the Magyar Defence Minister it, too, was titled 'Royal Hungarian' (k.u.). Each regimental headquarters and the regiment's number corresponded to that of the Area Command in which the unit had been formed.

Hungarian Landsturm regiments were formed for the Cavalry and Infantry arms, unlike the Austrian Landsturm which raised only Infantry. The proposed establishment of four battalions to a Hungarian regiment was seldom met and the number of regiments which existed in peacetime was increased by only one during the Great War.

However, conforming to the role of provincial, second line troops, independent battalions were raised for lines-of-communication duties and other, non-combatant tasks. These battalions bore two numbers; the second one was the number of the Landsturm Area Command in which they had been raised and the first number was that of the battalion. The 5th Area Command was Szeged and the Landsturm battalions raised in that Command would have been numbered 1/5, 2/5, 3/5 etc.

By September 1918 the number of Hungarian Landsturm regiments still in the Line was eight, of a total of thirty three.

6: Uniform

FOLLOWING Austria's defeat by Prussia in 1866, the changes carried out by the Imperial authorities included the adoption of dark blue as the colour of the infantry tunic, in place of the traditional white. The introduction of a pike-grey, combat dress, during 1907, promoted the blue uniform to the status of Parade and Walking Out Dress.

By the year 1915, the pike-grey uniform had become standard issue for all arms and other amendments to the clothing regulations simplified the uniform. Nevertheless, the longer the war continued the more difficult it became for the Imperial authorities to procure sufficient uniform material and, to cover the shortage, thousands of captured Italian jackets and trousers were adapted and issued. But even such makeshift measures could not make good the deficiencies and, even before the end of the war, the bulk of the Army was dressed in shoddy, unmatching and ill fitting oddments of uniform. The remark by a soldier from one of the depressed provinces of Bosnia to his officer, summarised the situation succinctly. 'We are not', said he 'a uniformed army of heroes, but a crowd of beggars'.

Before going on to describe the blue and grey uniforms it must be explained that Common Army Infantry regiments could only be identified by the correct grouping of the regimental facing colour, button colour and any other, special dress distinction like the fez or the Jäger cap. The facing colour was the most important of the means of identification. The spectrum did not allow each of the 102 regiments of the Line to have an individual colour and, in fact, to identify the regiments no more than nine colours were used and these were broken down into twenty eight shades. There were ten red, two brown, three yellow, six green, two blue, two grey, one black, one white and one hazel. No more than four regiments shared any one shade and two of these regiments were on the German and two on the Hungarian establishments. One German regiment and one Hungarian regiment wore buttons in yellow metal. The other German and Hungarian regiment wore buttons in white metal. The trouser style then determined which regiment was German and which was Hungarian.

Thus no more than one regiment of the Line had the same combination of facing colour, button colour and trouser pattern.

ABOVE: The Colour of the Maria Theresa Academy being paraded during a 'passing out' parade. The officer on the right of the Colour is a Field Officer in a Common Army Hussar regiment. The Ensign is wearing the blue Parade dress. The officer on the left of the picture is wearing the pike-grey Field Service uniform. He also wears on his left arm a black mourning band for the death of the Emperor.

PARADE DRESS
THE LINE INFANTRY'S UNIFORM

Tunic: This was a single-breasted garment fastened by six domed buttons of regimental pattern and marked with the regimental number. The stand-up collar, cuffs, shoulder straps and shoulder rolls were all in facing colour. The officer's tunic was also piped down the front, along the lower edge of the skirt, round the vent and the pockets at the back of the tunic. Officers' tunics were without shoulder straps.

In German regiments the cuff was of the simple turn-back pattern, but the Hungarian style was that of an inverted chevron. The Hungarian cuff also bore a distinctive device known as a 'bear's paw', in gold or silver for officers and in white cloth for other ranks.

Field and General Officer rank was indicated by a band of gold lace around the cuff. The top photograph on page 60 shows that sufficient of the cuff was left uncovered for the facing colour to be identified.

Non-commissioned officers who volunteered to extend their period of service were awarded a chevron of gold lace, half-inch wide, to be worn, inverted,

Detail of the Hungarian 'Bear's paw' cuff ornament. This could be in gold, silver, or white cloth depending on the regimental button colour and whether the wearer held commissioned rank or not.

above the left cuff. A second, third and fourth chevron in quarter-inch gold lace was awarded for three, six and nine years' service, respectively. The One Year Volunteer wore upon both cuffs a stripe of yellow silk centred with a thin black line. The Hungarian One Year Volunteer carried a chevron, conforming to the shape of his cuff, in black and yellow, while the Honved One Year Volunteer bore the same sort of chevron but with a central line in red.

Veterinary and Pharmacist One Year Volunteers were identified by a cuff band of lace in the colour and style of that worn on the shakos of Infantry Corporals.

Shako: The Parade Dress shako was of black felt, with the visor top and strap in black patent leather. A cockade of gold wire with a central circlet of black felt was worn above the centre of the head-dress. The Imperial Cypher was set upon the black felt central section of the cockade. The cockade for other ranks was a pressed brass disc with a black painted centre.

Rank was shown on the shako by borders of lace, one and a half inches wide. These were in gold for officers and in yellow for non-commissioned-officers. Officers also had a half-inch band of gold lace around the visor and a matt gold chain, one-eighth of an inch in diameter, around the bottom of the shako.

The shako plate showed the Imperial eagle; in gilded metal for officers and in brass for the rank and file.

Shako Lace Patterns
Officer's shako lace in gold

Field Officer's
also worn on sleeve

Captain

Lieutenant

Other Rank's lace in yellow

Lance Corporal's
shako cord

Sergeant or Senior NCO

Corporal

For Honved regiments the device shown was the Arms of Hungary with the motto, in Magyar or Croatian 'For King and Country'.

Trousers: For officers on the German and Hungarian establishments as well as for other ranks on the German establishment, pike-grey, or light blue slacks. Other ranks in Hungarian regiments wore a tight fitting trouser in light blue which was shaped to the leg. This garment was piped in yellow/black down the outside seam and on the thighs. This thigh piping took the form of inverted, Austrian knots. Mounted trumpeters of Infantry or Jäger regiments or battalions wore blue riding breeches and jackboots. These men as well as Landwehr, cadets and time serving NCO's were allowed to wear blue slacks when off duty.

Overcoats: The style for all ranks was a double-breasted, semi-belted garment of dark blue/grey cloth. Officers' overcoat collars were of dark blue velvet. All ranks wore collar patches, known as Parolis, in the regimental facing colour and for officers these patches were headed by a button. Officers'

Greatcoat collar patches, (Parolis) for; left, officer's and, right, other ranks.

coats were piped down the front edge and round the cuffs. Other ranks' coats were unpiped and had shoulder straps.

Greatcoats for all ranks were fastened by a double row of six domed buttons of regimental pattern.

There was also a pike-grey overcoat for officers, which was longer skirted than the blue but otherwise of the same cut. It had a velvet collar but was unpiped.

Other Dress Articles: A neck cloth, known as a stock, in black material with a white border, was fitted around the neck in such a way that the white edge showed behind the cut-away, stand-up collar.

Boots, shoes and equipment, were of black leather.

Gloves when worn were white.

All the above are applicable to the Parade Dress of all regiments of the Army.

THE JÄGER AND BOSNIAN UNIFORMS
JÄGER

Tunic: This was of the same pattern as the tunic of Line Infantry regiments but was coloured pike-grey. All pipings and coloured facings on the tunic were in green.

Landesschützen officers had a double-breasted tunic with a double row of eight buttons. They were further distinguished by shoulder straps on their tunics.

The plumed cap: The Jäger cap was similar in appearance to the British bowler hat and was made of black felt. The curling brim was edged in black patent leather. A wide cord, each end of which terminated in a woven acorn, was carried round the base of the crown and fastened at the back of the head. The cord and acorn was in gold for officers and in green for other ranks. On the left side of the cap was a holder into which was fitted a plume of dark green cock feathers. The holder and plume were held

RIGHT: The parade uniform of a Colonel of a Kaiserjäger regiment, showing the green facings on collar and cuffs, the Jäger cap and the officer's waist belt in yellow silk.

in place by a cap badge depicting a golden horn, within the wind of which was a silver Tyrolean eagle.

A black patent leather chin strap was adjusted by a brass buckle.

Trousers: For officers, pike-grey slacks with two wide green stripes down the outside leg. Landwehr and Landesschützen had a single, narrow stripe.

Jäger officers were authorised to wear close fitting riding breeches in blue-grey cloth or in buckskin.

Other ranks had slacks of the same pattern as well as artillery type trousers worn with high, cloth gaiters, piping on the trousers and a single thin green line.

Overcoats: Pike-grey for all ranks. Officers' coats piped in green.

BOSNIAN JÄGER

Wore standard Bosnian uniform (as described below) but in pike-grey with green facings.

LEFT: The cap of an officer of the Tyrolean Kaiser jäger, made of hard felt with patent leather trimmings. The dark green cocks' feathers held in place by the Jäger badge.

BOSNIAN REGIMENTS

Sky-blue jacket of Line Infantry pattern with red facings. The sky-blue trousers were distinctive in cut, fitting tight to the calf of the leg and being very wide cut from the calf to the waist.

Head-dress was a red fez with a blue tassel. Non-Muslim officers wore the standard shako.

HUNGARIAN LANDWEHR (HONVED) REGIMENTS

Tunic: Of dark blue cloth, double-breasted in cut with two rows, each of eight, yellow metal buttons. Other ranks' tunics were piped in red at the bottom and top of the collar. At the bottom of each sleeve was an inverted, Austrian knot in red lace. The shoulder straps, shoulder roll, vents and around the buttons in the skirt were also piped in red.

Officers' tunics were piped in the fashion of Line Infantry tunics and, in addition, the sleeves bore Austrian knots in gold lace.

The Honved officer's waist sash was of antique, Hungarian style—barred and with chains and tassels.

Trousers: Officers' trousers were of Line Infantry pattern but with red piping.

Other ranks wore the close fitting, Hungarian style trouser in deep sky-blue cloth. Piping was as for Line Infantry but in red.

UNDRESS UNIFORM— INFANTRY AND JÄGER (OFFICERS ONLY)

Tunic: Of pike-grey cloth, cut on the lines of the Field Service tunic but more closely fitting.

Shako: Black with a black leather peak and chinstrap. The chinstrap buckle was worn centrally and was fastened at either end by a small gilt button. Around the base of the cap was a double cord in black-flecked gold lace. At the front of the shako was a double loop of gold lace and down the centre of each loop a black line. Each loop was fastened by a button. At the top, centre of the cap a rosette.

Jäger officers wore a small horn upon the gold loop of their shako.

Trousers: These were known as Salonhosen, were black in colour and were piped down the outside seam of the leg in scarlet or green.

Buttons and Badges: The button colour did not only distinguish the regiments of the Army but could also indicate the differences in other formations.

Austrian Landwehr officers wore white metal buttons embossed with their regimental number in Arabic numerals. Other ranks carried the number on the shoulder strap in white, alpaca cloth.

Hungarian Landwehr (Honved) regiments had matt yellow, metal buttons.

Bosnian regiments and Feldjäger battalions had yellow metal buttons showing the unit number. Bosnian units had Roman numbers and Feldjäger battalions Arabic numerals.

Kaiserjäger, Bosnian Feldjäger and Grenzjäger had matt yellow, metal buttons.

Landesschützen units had white metal buttons embossed with their number in Roman figures.

The use of distinctive and individual regimental badges, in the sense of those worn by the British regiments, was not a normal feature of the Austrian Army and the only badge distinction between Line and Jäger units was the hunting or rifleman's horn worn by Jäger, Landwehr and Schützen regiments. This device, in gold, was worn in place of the upper button on the field service cap or, on the shako loop, in other uniforms (officers only).

Kaiserjäger and Kaiserschützen (formerly Landesschützen) regiments showed a silver, Tyrolean eagle in the wind of the horn, while Bosnian Feldjäger carried the Imperial eagle within theirs.

The other Feldjäger battalions and the Landwehr infantry regiments carried their battalion or regimental number within the wind of the horn; Feldjäger battalions with gold, Arabic figures and Landwehr regiments with silver, Arabic numbers.

ABOVE: Comparison between Parade Dress of dark blue tunic, piped in the regimental facing colour, black felt shako and pike-grey slacks with Service Dress of pike-grey, later field-grey overall, with no piping apart from the patch in facing colour.

SERVICE DRESS

By the end of the nineteenth century armies all over the world were becoming aware that modern war with its accurate, long range and destructive weapons could no longer be fought by lines or by solid blocks of soldiers exposed and distinctive in brightly coloured uniforms. A revision in infantry tactics together with the adoption of a neutral coloured, practical battle dress was long overdue and foreign forces began to follow the lead set by the British Army in selecting some dull, background tone for the colour of their field service uniform.

Austria-Hungary had been one of the first European nations to understand the necessity for concealment and had produced a grey, combat uniform for

 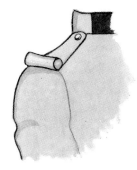

ABOVE LEFT: Field Service tunic in pike grey with concealed buttons and four flapped pockets. ABOVE RIGHT: Shoulder roll fitted to Field Service tunic. This helped to retain the rifle on the shoulder and prevented it from slipping off when marching.

the Jäger regiments of its Army. This colour was adopted for the standard service dress which was introduced in 1907. Certain national and service distinctions were preserved but the uniform became general issue for all arms by the year 1915. It was also in that year that a change in colour from pike-grey to field-grey was begun.

Tunic: This was a simple version of the blue, Parade Dress tunic. There were no coloured collars, shoulder straps or shoulder rolls and the small amount of piping which was retained was discarded during 1917. The most distinctive addition was of four, flapped pockets; two breast and two hip. A rise and fall collar replaced the stand-up collar during 1915. Another major change was the concealment of most of the tunic buttons. Those on the pockets were concealed under the decorative flaps and those fastening the jacket were hidden by a fly front.

Two oblong patches in regimental facing colour each two and three-quarter by one and a half inches, fitted on either side of the join. These replaced the collar in regimental facing colour. Upon these patches were worn the

BELOW: Two types of captured Italian tunics used by the Austro-Hungarian forces when supplies of material for their own tunics ran short.

Lettering style for unit indentification stencils

5
5th Common Army Infantry Regiment

TJ1
1st Regiment of Tyrolean Kaiserjäger

GrJ4
4th Grenzjäger battalion

J3
3rd Feldjäger battalion

KS1
1st Regiment of Kaiserschützen

Lsb4
4th Landsturm battalion

bh3
3rd Regiment Bosnia Herzingovinia

bhJ1
1st Battalion Bosnian Herzingovinian Jäger

stars of rank and, behind them, the badges of any specialist unit to which the wearer belonged. As a consequence of shortages in facing cloth the patches were reduced in size, during 1917, to two coloured strips, about half an inch wide, fitted two inches from the collar join. During the same year an order was issued by which only officers retained buttons in regimental colour. Other ranks were issued buttons in brown composition of cloth covered. Cap buttons were painted grey.

In 1917 shoulder straps were used, once again, to show regimental distinction; not by a reintroduction of facing colours, but by a system of affixing patches of American cloth (a coated linen) to the straps.

Five patches were issued to other ranks and one patch to the officers. Upon these patches (two for the tunic straps, two for the greatcoat straps and one for the cap) was stencilled the number and/or initials which identified the unit. On the shoulder straps, these patches were fastened in such a way that they could be read from the front.

The colour of the stencilled letters and numbers indicated the administration under which the unit served:

- Blue : Common Army Line and Bosnian regiments
- Pink : Hungarian Landwehr (Honved), and Austrian Landsturm.
- Grey or White : Hungarian Landsturm
- Green : Kaiserjäger, Kaiserschützen, Grenzjäger, Landwehr and, sometimes, Austrian Landsturm.

ABOVE: Battalion observation post on the Isonzo Front, August, 1917. Note the reduction of the collar patch to a narrow strip of cloth on the officers inside the post and on the right. Note also the unofficial cap badges. The seated officer is wearing the obsolete full patch. (IWM-Q64323).

Common Army Line regiments needed no identifying letter—their regimental number, in blue—was sufficient, but other formations required a letter or letters to distinguish them.

K S	:	Kaiserschützen
T J	:	Tiroler Kaiserjäger
b j	:	Bosnian Feldjäger
bh	:	Bosnian-Herzegovinian
LsB	:	Landsturm battalion
Gr J	:	Grenzjäger
J	:	Feldjäger

Head-dress: The field service shako for officers was a grey variant of the high crowned, black head-dress complete with gold loops down the front and the embroidered Imperial cypher upon a rosette, one and a half inches in diameter, placed above the centre of the cap. The wide bands of lace, indicating rank, were not worn on the grey shako but the black/gold chain round the bottom of the shako was retained.

The distinctive shape of this head-dress made the wearer an obvious target and this, together with its unsuitability for active service, led many officers in combat units to adopt the style of head-dress worn by the other ranks. This was a close fitting cap made of tunic material and fitted with a short peak in black composition material. This peak, like that of the officers shako, was often covered with grey cloth or paint. Above the centre of the cap was a circular badge in metal or papier mache bearing the Imperial cypher. The cap had ear flaps which buttoned under the chin and, when not used thus, were fastened at the front of the cap by two buttons of regimental pattern.

Other ranks' Field Service Cap with coated buttons and regimental number on a patch.

The Imperial Cypher badge worn on the front of the cap by other ranks of German regiments. When the Emperor Franz Josef died the Imperial Cypher became K—for the Emperor Charles. Magyar regiments carried a cap button IFJ and IK respectively.

Officer's field service cap with grey strap, gilt ornaments and unpainted peak. This type of cap seldom carried unit insignia.

Bosnian regiments wore a grey fez with a grey tassel.

On the cap was fitted the fifth (in the case of officers the single) patch as described above. This was worn on the left side of the cap, except for Kaiserjäger and Kaiserschützen units who carried a black cock feather on that side of their head-dress. The patch with the letters and numbers identifying them was, therefore, placed on the right side of the cap.

Sprigs of oak in summer, and of fir in winter, with which the Habsburg armies had traditionally decorated caps and regimental colours on ceremonial occasions or on active service, were among the official decorations worn on caps. Another was the stripe in red or green which indicated that the wearer

RIGHT: The grey Field Service cap. The top cap is the Infantry pattern and bears the patch of the 315 Landsturm battalion. The lower cap is that of a soldier of the 5th Honved Hussar regiment.

ABOVE: A decoration for bravery being pinned on a soldier wearing Field Service Marching Order and carrying the M95 rifle. Note the regimental number patch on the caps of the second and fourth soldiers in the line.

LEFT: An example of the winter camouflage cloak worn here by a sentry in the Tyrol in 1917.

RIGHT: Soldier on the Italian Front, during 1917, wearing the Austrian woollen cap-comforter.

ABOVE; TOP ROW: Different types of badges worn by the Austro-Hungarian forces. Kuk Feld Transport Leitung VI, 1914–1916 (Imperial and Royal Field Transport HQ VI). Surrounded by a wreath bearing the words 'Weltkrieg' (World War) as a superscription. A pair of winged wheels at the base of the badge. Size: 28 x 36 mm; Unofficial cap badge of the 17th Infantry Regiment. Brass, bearing a relief in profile of the Crown Prince, Franz Josef Otto, the date 24.XI.1916, and two armorial shields. Size: 26 x 36 mm; Miniature 42 cm shell made of hollow, yellow metal alloy. Shell case inscribed with the words 'A German greeting for our enemies, 1914' and an Iron Cross. Size: 40 x 20 mm; CENTRE: Paper. A portrait of the Crown Prince Franz Josef Otto framed by the words 'Empress Zita's Children's Day' and the date, 9th May, 1917. Size: 42 x 30 mm; BOTTOM ROW: Pressed light alloy relief of a wounded soldier surrounded by a wreath of oak and the dates 1914–1916. Size: 23 x 30 mm; Silvered alloy relief of Andreas Hofer. Fastening by a safety pin. Size: 22 mm; Bronze relief showing an armed soldier guarding a bridge and the legend 'Railway security, 1914–1916'. Fastened by a safety pin. Size: 30 x 21 mm.

had been wounded. These narrow, two-inch high stripes were worn on the left side of the cap and each strip of cloth denoted a wound received in action. The institution, during 1917, of a wound medal removed this form of decoration from head-dress.

Unofficial badges were made of a wide variety of materials and depicted many aspects of military life. Some were insignia of divisions, Corps or Armies with which the wearer had served, others marked the number of winters spent campaigning and some badges bore the likenesses of members of the Royal Family or of senior Army commanders.

ABOVE, TOP ROW: More unofficial badges: Relief in light alloy, zinc coloured, showing a ration train and tents in mountainous country. Superscribed: 'Imperial and Royal Rations Troops', and below the figures; 'World War, 1914–1918'. Fastened by a safety pin. Size: 40 x 43 mm; Relief in light alloy, zinc coloured. Portrait bust of the Emperor Charles surrounded by a laurel wreath, with the words Carolus Imp et Rex. Fastened by a safety pin. Size: 32 x 40 mm; Relief in light alloy, zinc coloured showing a lion crushing a snake. Superscribed: 'Offensive 1917–18 against Italy'. Fastened by a safety pin. Size: 44 x 33 mm; CENTRE: Medallion in zinc alloy. Circular. Black ribbon fastened on pin. Medallion bears the relief of the Emperor Franz Josef I in profile, above a laurel wreath and the dates of birth (1830) and his death (1916); BOTTOM ROW: Relief in zinc coloured alloy showing the rear view of a man advancing with a sword in his hand. On either side of the frame, two shields bearing the arms of Austria, Germany, Turkey and Bulgaria. Superscription in Cyrillic: 'Army Group Mackensen. Offensive against Rumania.' Fastened by a safety pin. Size: 30 x 36 mm; Relief in zinc coloured alloy. Profile of the Archduke Charles supported by two, antique, armed figures. Legend below the picture reads 'The Archduke Charles' Army Front, 1916'. Size: 30 x 36 mm; Hollow, light zinc alloy shield. 3rd Army. On the shield a sword and superimposed on this a cross and the dates 1916–1917. Fastened by a safety pin. Size: 44 x 22 mm.

BELOW, LEFT TO RIGHT: Oval, imitation pottery, showing a wounded soldier in bas-relief and coloured. Date shown as 1914–1916. Size: 20 x 25 mm; Circular, imitation pottery, Red Cross, 1914–1915–1916. Size: 22 mm; Oval, imitation pottery, showing, in relief, an angel protecting a wounded soldier and his family. Blue background, white figures. Size: 20 x 25 mm.

RIGHT: Austrian knot in slate grey worn on the Field Service trousers by Royal Hungarian Landwehr (Honved) troops.

Sleeve bands for Einjährig-freiwillige or one year volunteers. The straight band was worn in German regiments and the chevron pattern in Hungarian regiments.

In conditions of extreme cold two further types of head-dress were issued. The first of these was a grey woollen cap-comforter, which carried the Imperial cypher, and was worn in place of the service cap. The second was a toque worn, like the Balaclava helmet, under the cap.

Trousers: The basic pattern for German regiments of the Common Army, the Jäger, Landwehr and Landsturm was a pair of slacks (Pantalonen), piped along the seam of the outside leg and fastened at the ankle by a pair of buttons.

The Hungarian type was the normal, close fitting, Magyar pattern with a thigh knot of piping, in yellow for Line regiments, and in slate grey for Hungarian Landwehr (Honved) troops. As part of the move to standardise trouser design, the 1917 amendment to the clothing regulations abolished the thigh piping and ordered that the Hungarian establishment should wear trousers of the Common Army artillery pattern.

The artillery pattern was intended to be worn with leather gaiters fitting around the calf. The trouser was, therefore, shaped to the calf and then cut full above it. Variants of this pattern were worn by Bosnian regiments, Grenzjäger and Kaiserjäger units. The leather gaiter was peculiar to the artillery dress and Grenzjäger wore thick socks outside the legs of the trouser. Kaiserjäger wearing this pattern trouser had high, linen gaiters. Bosnians wore no special leg covering with this pattern trouser.

Another variant of the artillery pattern was worn by the Tiroler Landesschützen who wore socks of the pattern used by the Grenzjäger.

Officers had tended to wear riding breeches and boots but these latter were abandoned in favour of puttees. By the end of 1915 the bulk of the Imperial Army was wearing some form of puttee with their trouser style.

Coats: The field service greatcoat was the usual pattern, medium skirted, half belted, double-breasted garment with a turn back cuff. It fastened by two, slightly diagonal lines of buttons in regimental pattern. From 1917 the shoulder straps bore the American cloth patches described above and the collar had the usual Parolis in regimental facing cloth.

Landesschützen and Bosnian Grenzjäger were issued with a short cloak with attached hood. White camouflage cloaks were worn by Alpine units and others, during winter and when fighting in snowy country.

Other cold weather clothing included overcoats, double lined with fur or flannel, fur lined waistcoats and coats of animal skins. All these were issued to sentries or to men on outpost duty.

Footwear: Two sorts of lace-up boots were issued. The first was for ordinary duties; the second for active service in difficult country. When, towards the end of the war, insufficient supplies of leather were available to repair boots, a regulation was issued that only boots of infantry regiments were to receive special nailing and impregnating against wet. Boots of non-combatants were marked so that they did not receive this special treatment.

Officers wore riding boots, mountaineering boots or leather gaiters fastening by straps.

In conditions of extreme cold and wet the ordinary army boot offered little protecton against frostbite or trench foot and a number of improvisations were tried. These included overboots made of felt or of tarred straw.

BRASSARDS

These were in very common use in the Imperial Army.

The standard issue in black/gold was used to identify as a soldier of the Austrian Empire those who had not been issued with uniform. This brassard also served to identify civilians in Army service. Personnel of railway and telegraph units on the Austrian establishment had a similarly coloured armband as did military correspondents, whose band bore, in addition, the word 'Press'. The Hungarian establishment's transport troops brassard was red and carried rank badges and a double winged wheel in gold.

Selection of Brassards worn by the Austro-Hungarian Army

Standard Austrian.
Colours: Yellow/black/yellow

Tyrolean Standstutzen.
Colours: Green/white.
Worn in conjunction with standard Austrian brassard.

Standard Hungarian.
Colours: Green/white/red.

Railway and Telegraph troops.
Colour: Yellow band, black winged wheel.

Vets.
Colour: white band, brown star.

Telegraphists or Signals units.
Colour: Yellow band, black letter.

Red Cross and Medical Personnel.
Colour: White band, red cross.

RIGHT: Men of a regimental aid post wearing Red Cross brassards. Note also the high marching boots and the heavy studding in the soles clearly visible in this picture.

Another red brassard was that worn by members of the Order of St John and upon the red background was a white, Maltese cross. The Order of the Red Cross were identified by a white armband upon which was superimposed the insignia of their Order. Stretcher bearers and other medical personnel also wore a red cross armband.

Veterinary personnel had a brown star upon their white armband and political officials had a gold, metal, Imperial Cypher upon a white brassard. A dark blue brassard was worn by mountain guides and upon the blue background were the letters B F (Bergführer) with a vertical ice-pick between the letters.

A green and white brassard identified Tyrolean Standschützen and Hungarian Landsturm men were issued with an armband in the national colours—green, white and red.

Officers of foreign armies on tours of the Front were issued with a yellow armband with the word 'Attache', in black letters.

SPECIALIST AND INFANTRY PROFICIENCY BADGES

The most distinctive proficiency badge was the cord for marksmanship. These consisted of an aiguillette in red for Line Infantry marksmen, and in green for Jäger. This was the award for second-class shots. A gold aiguillette was awarded for first-class marksmen.

One end of the plaited cord aiguillette was fastened to a button inside the jacket and the other end to the shoulder strap. From this end there descended a cord to which was fixed five, wollen balls in red or green.

Other infantry badges for proficiency in judging distance, first aid and for marksmanship with machine-guns were worn on the right breast.

RIGHT: Collar badge of a Signals and Telegraph detachment; FAR RIGHT: Metal edelweiss worn by mountain troops and men of the Edelweiss Corps.

RIGHT: The distinctive aiguillette worn by marksman in red for Line infantry and green for Jäger. The plaited cord was in gold for first-class marksmen.

Distance-judging Badge for Infantry (*Distanzschätz-auszeichnung*).

Searchlight Units (*Scheinwerferabzeichen*).

Red Cross Badge (*Krankenpflege-auszeichnung für alle Truppen*).

Trench Mortar Units (*Minenwerferabzeichen*).

Carrying Units (*Trägerabzeichen*).

Entrenching Units (*Bauarbeiterabzeichen*).

Cyclist Units (*Radfahrerabzeichen*).

Electrical Units (*Elektroabzeichen*).

ABOVE: A selection of Infantry badges stamped from brass worn on the right breast by various specialised units indicating their function, and ordinary infantry for proficiency in certain tasks.

ABOVE: The Schwarzlose machine-gun, without shield, being used by men of an Infantry machine-gun section. Note the machine-gun badge worn by all three men on the right-hand side of their caps.

BELOW RIGHT: Close up of the machine-gunner's cap badge. BELOW LEFT: Other rank's and machine-gunner's metal collar badge. The officer's badge was of woven metal lace.

BELTS, SASHES AND SWORD KNOTS

One of the visible, easily recognisable distinctions of an Imperial officer was the yellow silk sash, marked with two thin black lines and terminating in two heavy embroidered tassels. This sash was usually worn round the waist and fastened at the left hip. The waist sash tassels bore on the obverse an Imperial eagle and on the reverse, the Imperial cypher.

All decorative sashes, which were also worn on active service, were discarded by Army order, during September, 1914.

The leather waist belt for all ranks was fastened by a large, square, brass buckle. That for officers bore the Imperial cypher; other ranks' buckles were stamped with the Imperial eagle. Ensigns were, sometimes, permitted to wear the wide cavalry belt which fastened by the tongue and prong method.

RIGHT: The tassels on the officer's waist sash showing the embroidered eagle and Cypher.

Officers' sword slings were of red Morrocco leather, faced with gold lace and having a central line in black. The sword knot was of gold thread showing on reverse and obverse the same devices as on the waist sash tassels. Ensigns had sword knots of yellow and gold silk and, for non-commissioned officers from Corporal to Ensign, the bayonet knot was in yellow cotton. Bandmasters sword knots were in silver thread and all bandsmen, including non-commissioned officers, had bayonet knots in white thread worked with the regimental facing colour.

Badges of rank

Field-Marshal	Gold-lace in wave pattern
Colonel-General	Three silver stars set triangularly in a silver laurel wreath
General	Three silver stars and broad gold lace
Lieutenant-General	Two silver stars and broad gold lace
Major-General	One silver star and broad gold lace
(All the above badges were imposed on a red ground)	
Colonel	Three stars (of opposite colour to the buttons) and broad gold or silver braid (same colour as the buttons)
Lieutenant-Colonel	Two stars and broad braid (as described above)
Major	One star and broad braid (as described above)
(Staff officers wore their ordinary badges of rank imposed upon a background which agreed with the colour of their buttons)	
Captain	Three stars of the same colour as the buttons
Lieutenant	Two stars of the same colour as the buttons
2nd Lieutenant	One star of the same colour as the buttons
Ensign	One silver star on gold braid
Cadet	Celluloid stars on gold braid
(The cadet has no rank but carries the same number of stars as the rank he held on becoming a cadet ie, a Sergeant wore three stars)	
Sergeant Major	Three celluloid stars and yellow silk braid
Sergeant	Three celluloid stars
Corporal	Two celluloid stars
Lance-Corporal	One celluloid star
(Two unusual ranks in the Austro-Hungarian Army were held to be the equivalent of junior officer rank without the authority)	
Deputy Officer (Offizierstellvertreter)	Celluloid star on silver braid
Staff Non-commissioned Officer	Three celluloid stars on a yellow stripe, surmounted by gold braid

7: Arms and Equipment

THE infantry regiments of the Austro-Hungarian Army entered upon the Great War with a maximum of eight machine-guns per regiment and with the greatest number of their men using rifles. Within four years the firepower which the regiments controlled had risen to a potential inconceivable in peacetime including, as it did, infantry guns for close support in attack and defence, trench artillery pieces of varying calibres, assault machine pistol sections and hand machine-gun detachments. Communication within the regiment had improved through the expansion and improvement of the telephone and wireless organisation, rock-drilling units of the regimental technical company had excavated strong fortifications in the mountains of the southern alps and searchlight sections illuminated no-man's-land to detect enemy offensive movement.

The Army had developed within four years to a position where shortages of men had nearly been balanced by the increased destructive capabilities of newer weapons. Militarily, it was a long way from the army and the tactics which had prevailed at the outbreak of the war.

RIFLES, CARBINES AND PISTOLS

The most common of the rifle types with which the infantry regiments were issued in 1914 was the 8mm (·315 inch), Mannlicher M 95. This was a breech action, straight bolt, magazine fed rifle weighing 8lb. Length without bayonet, was 4 feet 2 inches. The magazine held five rounds and, together with the trigger guard, formed one complete part of the rifle. The sight was the conventional blade and leaf pattern. The backsight was fitted to a sliding bed graduated, in paces, for distances up to 2,500 yards. A battle sight was zeroed for 410 yards.

The M 90, which had been made obsolete by the introduction of the M 95, was the weapon usually issued to Landsturm units. The stock and barrel were the same as for the M 95, but there were certain differences in the breech mechanism and in the fitting of the bayonet. There was also an additional blade foresight fitted onto the upper sling swivel. This was used in conjunction with a sliding attachment on the backsight, for ranges between 1900 and 2500 yards. The most effective range of this weapon was between 500 and 1500 yards.

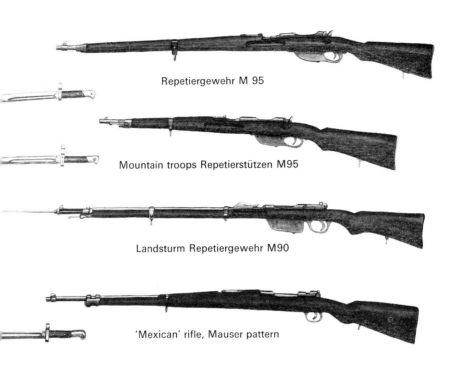

Repetiergewehr M 95

Mountain troops Repetierstützen M95

Landsturm Repetiergewehr M90

'Mexican' rifle, Mauser pattern

The M7 repeating pistol. This weapon held ten rounds which were loaded into the butt from a charger.

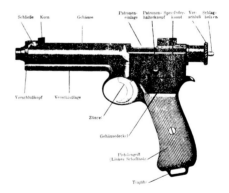

Two shorter versions of the M 95 were issued for mountain troops. These were known as the M 95 carbine and the M 95 Stützen. The carbine weighed 7lb 12oz and was 39½ inches long: the Stützen was 7lb 14oz in weight and 40 inches long. The Stützen had a wooden upper forestock and the carrying sling fitted below the rifle. The carbine was carried by a sling which fitted on the side of the weapon. Otherwise the weapons were identical. The carbine when fitted with a bayonet had a tendency to fire high and, to counteract this, an additional foresight was placed on the bayonet boss. Both shorter versions of the M 95 were ranged for distances between 500 and 1900 yards.

Mauser rifles manufactured for the Mexican government and commandeered at the outbreak of the war, were issued but then withdrawn when a sufficient supply of M 95s became available. The Mauser fired a 7mm (·276 inch) calibre bullet.

All the Mannlicher weapons fired M 93 ammunition; brass cased with a round nosed bullet usually carried in clips of five. The muzzle velocity of the M 90 and M 95 was 2030 feet per second. The muzzle velocity of the carbine and Stützen was 1900 feet per second.

The standard repeating pistol was the M 7, a 7·9mm (·311 inch) calibre weapon weighing $2\frac{1}{4}$lb, unloaded. The overall length was 9 inches.

The magazine held ten rounds which were loaded, from a charger, into the butt of the pistol. When the charger was withdrawn the pistol was automatically loaded. The rate of fire for this weapon was claimed to be 100 rounds per minute. Production of this weapon ceased in 1917.

SWORDS AND BAYONETS

The swords issued to the infantry were of two patterns; standard and mountain troop. The standard infantry officer's sword, was a polished steel weapon with a slightly curved, polished blade 32 inches long. At a point of the blade it was double edged and for the greater part of its length the blade was channelled. The combined weight of the sword and scabbard was 1lb 14oz. Swords of this type were issued to officers, ensigns and sergeants. It was designated M 61.

The M 61 infantry sword was on issue to non-commissioned officers, musicians, regimental drummers, artificers and medical personnel. This weapon had a pronounced curve and was made of unpolished steel. The blade was shorter (26 inches in length), but in every other respect was identical to the officer's weapon. The scabbard was of black leather attached to a frog. The weight of the weapon complete with scabbard was 1lb 14oz.

Mountain troops, both commissioned and non-commissioned were issued with short swords, just under 24 inches long. The officer's issue was recognisable by the piercing of the guard into the design of a double eagle and Imperial cypher. The other rank's side arm was unpierced.

The bayonet which fitted the M 95 rifle had a $9\frac{1}{2}$ inches long blade and weighed $12\frac{1}{2}$oz. It was carried in a metal sheath painted grey. This type of bayonet was fixed to the rifle by a fastening ring and a slide which fitted under the barrel as opposed to the M 90 bayonet which was attached to the left side of the weapon. This bayonet was $9\frac{3}{4}$ inches long. Sheath of the same type as for the M 95.

LEFT: Officer's pattern sword.

RIGHT: M 61 pattern Infantry sabre.

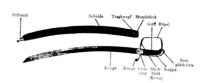

Both types of bayonet were double edged at the point and were deeply channelled to lessen the weight. On the head of the bayonet, near the release button, was the numeral indicating the type of rifle to which it fitted. Bayonets for non-commissioned officers were fitted with an attachment for the sword knot and the quillon was deeply curved.

It would be more accurate to describe the Pioneer's sword as a sword-bayonet-tool for, in addition to its use as a hand weapon it was also intended to perform certain, simple pioneer tasks. The M 53, which was on issue at the outbreak of the war, weighed $3\frac{1}{2}$lb complete with scabbard and

RIGHT: M 53 Pioneer sword-bayonet with scabbard.

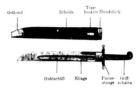

was 18 inches long. The sheath was of leather covered wood. The M 15 which replaced the M 53 was shorter and lighter by two inches and 4oz respectively. The scabbard was of mild steel painted grey.

In common with most armies the Austrians had entered the war wearing swords but the prevailing conditions of the war made the carrying of such side arms unnecessarily dangerous and impractical. The wearing of infantry swords ceased from January 15, 1917 and all ranks wore a bayonet with the correct sword knot for each regiment.

STEEL HELMETS AND OTHER ARMOUR

Once they had been introduced, steel helmets passed quickly into general service with the armed forces of the Western combatant nations, but Austria was the last of these major Powers to afford such protection to her soldiers and it was not until late in 1917 that a distinctively Austrian head piece was proposed. Steel helmets in the Austrian service were not on general issue and supplies were reserved for front line infantry units and storm troop detachments.

Initially Austrian troops were issued with German helmets, and many of these 1916 pattern pieces remained in service until the end of the war. The shape of this light (2lb $10\frac{1}{2}$oz) helmet afforded a greater depth of protection to the wearer than did the helmets issued by the Allied Powers. Austrian versions of the German 1916 and 1918 pattern helmets were produced and are almost indistinguishable from the German originals. The slight differences are to be found in the shape of the peak and in the flare of the neck guard. The Austrian version of the German 1918 pattern weighed 3lb 1oz, was $6\frac{3}{4}$ inches high, 12 inches long and $9\frac{3}{4}$ inches wide.

Inside the helmet was a three-quarter inch wide felt sweat band, fastened to the metal at three points by screws or rivets. Rising from, and fastened to the sweat band were three, wide triangular calf leather sections which fastened inside the crown by a cord. Between these leather sections and the metal of the crown was a number of pads, usually field dressings, which helped to cushion the head. The chin strap was made of half-inch webbing, passed through a pair of stirrups (in the 1918 pattern only). Strap adjustment was effected by a zinc buckle. On either side of the exterior of the helmet was a metal lug which supported a heavy, armoured brow plate. These metal pieces,

5 to 7lb in weight, unbalanced the wearer and were, therefore restricted to snipers.

The Austrian helmet proposed in 1918 but never generally introduced was quite unlike those which had preceded it and contained several unusual and easily recognisable features: a ventilator in the crown, a distinctive peak, no external lugs and a shallow step between the peak and the neck guard.

The helmet shape was that of a deep bowl the front rim of which was raised to form a distinctively angular peak which made a shallow step, only three-quarters of an inch higher than the neck guard. Helmet dimensions were: height $6\frac{1}{4}$ inches, length $11\frac{3}{4}$ inches, width 10 inches. Weight 2lb 14oz.

Interior padding and chin strap as above.

A small cross was cut through the top of the helmet and the metal then raised proud so that it supported a one inch diameter metal disc. This was fastened to a second disc within the helmet. Ventilating air entered through the gaps in the proud metal. The external disc acted, not only as the cover to this ventilator, but as a support for a brow plate which was retained in position by a wide leather or elastic band fastened around the base of the crown.

ARMOURED SHIELDS

Among the equipment adopted with the intention of reducing casualties to assaulting troops was the hand held shield, but these proved too cumbersome and too heavy for practical use.

An adaptation of these was the set shield used to reinforce static strong points. Supplies of these shields were issued from the end of 1916 and the dimensions were 24 x 18 inches. A slot, 2 x 6 inches, was cut from the metal. Weight was around 30lb The 1918 pattern weighed 50lb, was 26 x 12 inches and had a slot 2 x 5 inches. This shield was not supported by a metal strut as the 1916 pattern had been, but was kept upright by hinged metal cheek plates.

Large numbers of 'Ansaldo' body armour plates, captured from the Italians, were also used by the Austrians and were considered to be more serviceable

LEFT: Austrian steel helmet of the German pattern showing the large lugs intended to hold a metal visor. BELOW LEFT: Side view of the same helmet. Note the rivets for retaining the internal padding. BELOW RIGHT: Austrian ventilator pattern steel helmet.

than the native ones because they could be used either as body armour, as a portable shield, or as an armoured, set shield for a rifleman.

BODY ARMOUR

There was no native development of body armour and in the few instances of its use the Austrians used the German sets of four, overlapping plates covered by cloth and lined with felt pads. Three of these hung free while the fourth fastened to the body by canvas straps. The four plates, whose combined weight was between 19–22lb, were connected by webbing straps.

The use of such heavy and restricting armour, which could be worn to protect either the chest or the back, was confined to sentries on outpost duty and to men of assault, machine-gun detachments.

GAS MASKS

These were very much like the German pattern, being made in three sizes, and consisting of an impermeable, rubber treated face piece into which was screwed a drum packed with chemicals. The eye-pieces or windows were made of celluloid and an anti-dimming stick was issued.

The early pattern mask was not completely efficient, for it caused difficulties in breathing and these prevented the wearer from carrying out any other activity than firing a rifle.

An improved version was introduced during 1918.

The mask, together with a spare anti-gas drum, was carried in a metal container.

BELOW: Three different types of gas masks used by the Austro-Hungarian forces. The centre one is not specifically a gas mask, although it was used as such, and is in fact a type of oxygen breathing apparatus used for mining rescues.

RIGHT: A method of projecting grenades other than throwing them by hand is the use of a discharger fitted to the standard M 95 infantry rifle. The method of firing such a weapon is here demonstrated by an NCO. Note the bag containing more grenades under his left arm.

Another type of oxygen breathing apparatus was not intended as a personal, anti-gas, piece of equipment but was a rescue apparatus used, chiefly, in mining rescues. It was, however, frequently used in cases of severe gas poisoning.

HAND GRENADES

Until the adoption of the German stick grenade the bombs in the Austrian service were primitive and uncertain explosive devices. The two basic types were the conventional egg type and the Rohr grenade. This latter was a short,

LEFT: A soldier of a Common Army infantry regiment throwing a hand grenade. Italian Front, early 1916. Note also the camouflage face mask.

ABOVE: A Schwarzlose M 7/12 machine-gun fitted with the hinged shield in action on the Italian Front, 1915.

cast iron cylinder (rohr), four inches long. It was enclosed within a cardboard tube which also acted as a form of handle. The weight of the bomb was 1lb 13oz and incorporated a four or eight-second friction fuse. The maximum distance over which it could be thrown was 40 feet.

The first issue of hand grenades to the Austrian Army was made on March 1, 1915.

Percussion and tear gas bombs were also used.

MACHINE-GUNS

The standard issue machine-gun was the tripod mounted, Schwarzlose M 7/12 with a hinged, protective shield. This water-cooled weapon had a rate of fire of between 450 and 500 rounds per minute. The weight of the weapon complete with shield and tripod was 170lb: barrel 40lb, mounting 40lb, and shield 90lb. The shield was made of steel plate 7mm thick. Ammunition fired was the standard M 95 in belts of 250 rounds feeding from standard metal boxes.

The gun could be used in any one of three positions. Using the telescopic leg mounting at full extension the weapon stood some two feet above the ground and was then a normal medium/heavy automatic weapon. By completely retracting the legs the weapon could be fired at ground level. The use of the M 16 turntable, enabled the gun to be used as a long range, heavy machine-gun firing at distances greater than the normal 2,650 yards. Angle of fire for the normal mounting was 33 degrees lateral and 40 degrees of elevation and depression.

ABOVE: Men of an Alpine unit with the Schwarzlose M 7/12 medium machine-gun. Note that on this weapon the heavy hinged shield has been removed to save weight.

At the outbreak of war the organisation of a machine-gun company in an infantry regiment was of four sections each of two guns. The company commander and his four section commanders were commissioned ranks. The rank and file numbered 157 of whom 64 manned the guns, 9 were in reserve. A further 46 men were pack animal drivers. Twenty-four mules, sixteen horses and seven waggons were on the company strength. The whole force was divided into two echelons: the battle squadron and the ammunition train. In the battle squadron were all the officers, 80 men and all the pack animals. One mule carried the gun and 500 rounds, a second mule portered 2000 rounds of ammunition while a third carried the gun shield. The fourth and fifth animals of each section carried extra ammunition while the sixth, portered a tool kit and extra ammunition.

The second echelon contained four pairs of horse-drawn ammunition carts and two armourers' waggons. A total of 96,000 rounds of ammunition per company were carried on the carts. The telephonists, one supply waggon and the cooks' cart accompanied the ammunition train.

Schwarzlose M 7/12 with hinged shield and tripod mount.

Schwarzlose M 7/12 in the light machine-gun role with shield and tripod removed—mounted on a detachable tripod with butt added.

LEFT: No 1 mule of the machine-gun train carrying the barrel on the right side, the tripod on the left and the ammunition boxes on the top of the pack saddle. The rest of the train animals would carry additional ammunition, spare parts and a tool kit.

The company establishment of a mountain unit was 3 officers, 182 men and 44 pack animals. A lower scale of ammunition was carried and all this ammunition, the guns, cooking equipment and supplies were carried by the pack animal train. There were no carts on this establishment.

The increasing importance of the machine-gun on the battlefield demanded that the numbers of these weapons under regimental control be increased. This was done, as indicated in Section 3, so that, in addition to the machine-gun companies within a regiment, there were also light machine-gun sections within companies.

When the increase in machine-gun establishments was introduced and the fourth platoon of each company converted into two, light machine-gun sections, these platoons each contained 1 officer and 35 other ranks. Each platoon controlled four light machine-guns; stripped down versions of the M 7/12. The shield and tripod were discarded and the gun mounted on a detachable bipod and fitted with a shoulder butt. This type of weapon was classified as light and mobile and could be carried by a five-man team using special packs although it was usually brought forward by one of the two carts on the platoon establishment. A total of 104 men formed the battle echelon and 32 men the ammunition train. Everything was manhandled and not the least

BELOW: Men of a Common Army machine-gun company in a well prepared position on the Eastern Front. The No 1 on the gun is armed with the 07 pistol. The machine-gun troops insignia can be seen on the collar of the soldier on the right of the picture.

ABOVE: A posed picture demonstrating the team required for an Infantry gun and the ease with which it could be towed.

important was the water which these weapons used up very quickly, for after 1200 rounds of rapid firing the jacket had to be refilled.

Tactically the section controlling a pair of guns was the basic organisation and it was not usual for the guns of a section to be used individually, for they were intended to be mutually supporting.

The men of the machine-gun company and the machine-gun platoons were armed with carbines and bayonets. Officers and the Nos 1 on the guns had pistols.

Other machine-guns in use by the Imperial Army were the M 4 Maxim, used in siege warfare and the M 93 Skoda, used in fixed armoured positions. Trials were carried out during 1917 with the Bergmann gun but these trials were not successful and it was not until the last year of the war that a light, new type of automatic weapon was brought into service. This was the assault pistol, consisting of two, linked barrels, each with a magazine holding 20 rounds of 9mm ammunition. This weapon was carried into action by a two-man team and weighed 17lb when ready for action. The regulations for the pistol stressed that it was not intended to be used as a substitute machine-gun but that its main purpose was in defence, in a mobile role, to bring down a curtain of fire where it was most needed. It was, however, frequently used in infantry assaults.

THE INFANTRY GUN

The infantry gun was introduced into service during 1915 not, as it was stressed, to be a substitute for artillery but to be used in close support work both in defence and attack and to be used in counter battery fire. These guns were, therefore, short range weapons with a maximum range of 1968 yards and with a normal rate of fire of eight shots per minute, although this could be raised to sixteen with a well trained crew.

3·7 cm Skoda L 310, M 1915 Infantry Gun

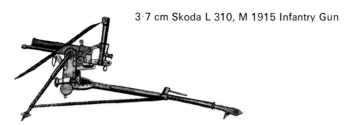

The gun weighed 124lb, and fired four sorts of ammunition. The first was a high explosive shell (M 15 and 16), weighing 19½oz and exploding on impact. The second had a detonating head which threw the body of the shell upwards upon exploding. This body then burst at a height of six feet above the ground. The third type of shell was the normal shrapnel projectile and the last was the star shell.

Each regiment had a section of infantry guns attached and this pair of 3·7cm, Skoda L 310, M 1915 weapons was controlled by a subaltern officer with an aspirant officer as his second-in-command. The No 1 on the gun was served by a six-man crew and included in the section was an armourer, three telephonists, two Corporals as reserves for the Nos 1, four pack animal drivers, and ammunition numbers. The normal establishment was 28 all ranks. The officers and the Nos 1 on the guns were armed with the repeating pistol, all the other personnel had carbines and bayonets. All the members of the infantry gun section were drawn from the infantry and given a special course of training.

New types of infantry gun including the 4·3 cm and the 4·7 cm (M 17) were tested during 1917 but did not come into general service.

Technical information   Calibre   37mm (1·457 inches)
                           Length   12·4 calibres.
                           Weight   56 kilo. (123·46lb)
                           Elevation   —10 to +60 degrees
                           Range   1800 metres (1968 yards)

TRENCH ARTILLERY

The Imperial authorities differentiated between the two types of ammunition fired by trench artillery pieces. Projectiles were either 'bomben' (defined as thin walled containers with at least one-third of their total weight in explosive), or as 'granaten' (thick walled containers with a sixth of their total weight in high explosive).

The weapons which fired these missiles were either Minenwerfer (which fired 'bomben') and Granatenwerfer (which projected 'granaten'). Two methods of firing were used; by explosive charge or by compressed air. The 1917 manual for weapon instruction (Waffenwesen. Instruktionsbuch für Reserveoffiziersschulen, 3rd Part), preferred the compressed air projection for the fact that it was both silent and invisible, giving neither the sound of a detonation when being fired, nor a cloud of smoke or flame.

The object of these weapons, according to the Manual, was to supplement the artillery by giving close support fire in cases where the distance between the respective trench lines made accurate firing by conventional artillery dangerous for the front line infantry. The mortar was described as a weapon of precision with a greater blast area than rounds of similar calibre fired by the artillery.

ABOVE: Men of a Common Army regiment beating off an Italian attack using rifle fire and trench mortars. A light (8 cm) projector is seen here before firing a 9 lb missile at short range.

In infantry regiments light Granatenwerfer ranged from 8cm to 10·5cm and medium projectors from 12–17cm. The light granatenwerfer weighed $37\frac{1}{2}$lb, and fired a 9lb cigar-shaped finned bomb over a distance between 98 yards (elevation 85 degrees) and 700 yards (elevation 45 degrees).

The 9cm medium Granatenwerfer projected a $52\frac{1}{4}$lb bomb distances of between 360 yards (elevation 45 degrees) and 87 yards (elevation 85 degrees). Ther heavy weight of this piece of ordnance (300lb) meant that it could only be carried for short distances by four men. Usually it was brought forward on a horse-drawn cart.

BELOW: A close up picture of the 9 cm mortar in a protected position. The bomb is being loaded into the breech of the piece by the man in the centre. Note that the piece can be broken down into parts for ease of transport.

ABOVE: The Austrian 9 cm mortar in a prepared position on the Southern Polish Front. Note the swabbing stick at the left side of the piece.

The 12cm Minenwerfer M 16 and M 17 projected the missiles by pneumatic pressure. In both cases the weapon weighed 154lb and broke down into barrel, base plate and bipod. Like all pneumatic mortars the angle of elevation was fixed and alterations in range were effected by increases or reductions in the air pressure. The weapon cannot be classified as light and mobile for, together with its equipment of compressed air cylinders and telephones, was transported in seven carts. The M 16 bomb weighed $10\frac{3}{8}$lb and that of the M 17 $15\frac{1}{2}$lb.

The 9cm M 15 and M 16 Minenwerfer were similar to the pneumatic M 17 but had no baseplate or traversing gear. The disadvantage of the M 15 and 16 was the large flame and cloud of smoke discharged when being fired. The Minenwerfer weighed 88·2lb and broke into two pieces for transport. The bombs fired were cylindrical, that of the M 15 weighing $12\frac{3}{4}$lb was base fused, the M 16 bomb was nose fused and weighed $24\frac{1}{4}$lb.

A detachment consisted of two sections controlling two projectors and the strength of the detachment depended upon the weight of the Minenwerfer

BELOW: A Kaiserschützen officer watches as a bomb is loaded into a well dug-in 40 cm mortar. Italian Front, 1917.

ABOVE: Sappers of an Infantry regiment's technical company, protected by armoured shields, prepare a defensive position by consolidating a mine crater with barbed wire obstructions.

and the type of country in which it was to be used. Usually the detachment had a strength of 30 men made up of a subaltern officer, two non-commissioned officers and ten men in the crews and the remainder of drivers, telephonists and an armourer.

Some of the lighter mortars were mounted on wheeled carriages but in most cases they were carried by their crews from the point where the cart had deposited the pieces.

THE PIONEER SECTION

As a result of the tactical reorganisation dictated by the course of the war a Technical Company, formed in each infantry regiment, not only took over the tasks of the Pioneer Section but was also equipped with special assault weapons. The strength of such companies fluctuated between 200 and 250 men but was usually, 5 officers, 213 other ranks, 35 horses, 6 pack animals and 15 carts. In independent battalions the strength was about 100 officers and men.

In 1914 the regimental pioneer detachment had consisted of 1 officer, 8 non-commissioned officers and 64 other ranks. The section had carried the field equipment of mining and woodworking tools and had been accompanied by a single pack animal loaded with explosives.

By 1918 the Technical Company had become a large, compact group of proficient men armed with a number of powerful weapons and sophisticated equipment. It was organised thus:

Company Commander, a senior NCO, the Train Commander, smiths, trumpeters, one corporal and four stretcher bearers together with some runners formed the headquarters group. There was then as many technical platoons as there were battalions in the regiment. In addition there was a heavy weapons platoon, a battle and a baggage train.

A Technical Platoon contained a Commander, a long service NCO, four Corporals, 36 men, a cook and a batman. There was an equipment cart in which were loaded the tools for wood cutting and excavation. An explosives cart carried 12 charges of $2\frac{1}{4}$lb weight and two 21lb charges, 70 detonators,

ABOVE: 45 cm searchlight detachment going into the line, (Italy, 1915).

and other explosive materials, 100 Verey light pistol cartridges (50 white and 50 coloured), 50 signal rockets and three boxes of hand grenades. Bridge building equipment was carried by some platoons on an extra cart, and all platoons were able to build roads, tunnels and to establish fortifications in the solid rock of the Alps.

The heavy weapons platoon contained a Commander, two searchlight sections, one heavy mortar (Minenwerfer) section and one light mortar (Granatenwerfer) section. A flame thrower section, one groom, one batman and a cook completed the platoon. Each section was commanded by a long service non-commissioned officer.

The first searchlight section contained an NCO and 9 men who controlled two 30cm (12 inch) lights for illuminating the immediate area in front of the trenches, up to a range of 400 yards. These lights were carried in cases, by four pack animals.

The second searchlight section of an NCO and 9 men controlled two 45cm (18 inch) lights which illuminated the ground in front of defensive positions and which were used in collaboration with machine-guns and the infantry gun detachments. These lights had a range of 1000 yards. A pair of carts brought the lights forward into position.

Regulations controlling the exposure of the beam were very strict and in no case, except that of any enemy night attack of major proportions, were the lights to be exposed for long periods. Movement of the beam across the ground was effected by a control system erected some distance to the side of the light.

The heavy mortar section contained an NCO and 9 men who worked a pair of 9cm ($3\frac{1}{2}$ inch) projectors as well as an NCO and four men with a 12cm ($4\frac{3}{4}$ inch) mortar. The 9cm projector had an ammunition supply of 36 rounds of $2\frac{1}{4}$lb missiles, 6 rounds of 5lb bombs, 6 incendiary grenades and 6 gas bombs. Signal flares and pistols were carried.

The ammunition supply for the 12cm mortar consisted of 15 rounds, the projectors and their bombs were carried into action in two carts. The light mortar section controlled four projectors which, together with ammunition, were loaded in one cart. Ammunition carried amounted to six boxes each

RIGHT: A static flame-thrower showing the long discharge tube and flexible hose. Most Austrian flame-throwers were part of the fixed defences of a trench.

of six rounds and eight boxes of four rounds. In addition hand grenades were carried.

The flame thrower detachment, consisting of a pair of projectors, was manned by a detachment of ten soldiers. The throwers were usually fixed into the wall of the trench system and were considered to be defensive weapons. Three types were in use and the flame projected carried for distances between 30 and 40 yards.

With the battle train rode the Paymaster and accompanying the train were the cook's cart, the repair cart and a mobile kitchen.

COMMUNICATIONS

At the outbreak of the war each platoon in a regiment had a three-man signals section; the patrol leader, who was also the writer, an observer and a signaller. This group was equipped with two flags; one white and the other, either red, blue, yellow or white/red. A collapsible mast completed the platoon signalling equipment, which weighed $3\frac{1}{2}$lb, and was carried on the outside of the knapsack.

On the company establishment there were two types of signalling lamp; an acetylene and a paraffin as well as a telephone section, again of three men, whose equipment was usually carried within the company cart in a special telephone chest. The field telephone equipment contained a combined speaking and listening head-set which could be used to send messages in Morse code. The usual amount of wire carried was just under a mile in length.

By 1917 the regimental telephone platoon had increased to a strength of 1 officer, 100 to 130 men and five carts. The regimental headquarters section contained 12 men and 1 cart, each of the battalion groups 24 men and a cart. There was a group of runners varying in strength between 13 to 17 men, exclusive of mounted messengers.

ABOVE: A Signals Section dug-out on Mount Rombou showing the standard telephone hand-piece and extension ear-piece. The rifle outside the dug-out is a Mexican Mauser. Note also the badges on the nearest man's cap, including a Cross of Bohemia and a portrait of the Emperor. (IWM-Q64320).

FIELD POST OFFICES

Each unit in the Austrian Army was given a code number and mail for the unit bore this Field Post number. Military centres behind the Front and battle fronts were given their own special number.

Lists of the units and their respective Field Post numbers were published, at intervals, in civilian newspapers.

MEDICAL

In a four battalion regiment there were seven doctors on establishment. This number reduced to five in a regiment of three battalions.

The establishment in a three battalion regiment was; 1 Medical Officer, 12 orderlies, 6 assistants, 48 stretcher bearers and 3 pack animals. Four stretcher bearers formed a company medical section and their equipment included two stretchers, splints and a first aid bag for each man.

In mountain regiments and Alpine detachments this establishment and the number of stretcher bearers was double the numbers quoted above.

OTHER EQUIPMENT

By 1917 a linen rucksack had generally replaced the two-part hide pack. The rucksack was about 27 inches wide by 21 inches high, made of stout linen and with two external pockets.

Shortages in leather stopped the production of bayonet frogs, spade and pick covers and cartridge pouches. These items were then made of imitation leather, webbing or in alloy. Infantry ammunition pouches were remodelled and formed a single (cavalry pattern) instead of the double pouch.

Infantry Equipment

Infantry pick in carrier.

Infantry entrenching tool in carrier.

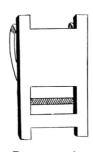 

Two types of portering frame for, at left, machine-gun and mortar ammunition and, at right, for standard rifle ammunition.

Cooking utensils and the water bottle were made of enamelled alloy. It was proposed to redesign the infantry water bottle so that it held one and a quarter pints of liquid.

Tents followed the German pattern and neither the material nor the colour conformed to the regulations.

All metal parts, which had been made in iron, were replaced by zinc parts and then by alloy. These metal parts were then reduced in size to save metal. Infantry belt buckles were replaced by tongue and buckle pattern cavalry buckles.

REGIMENTAL COLOURS

The number of Colours borne by each infantry regiment of the Imperial Army was reduced to one and this was in most cases that of the first battalion. Some regiments whose second battalion had particularly distinguished itself were permitted to retain that battalion's colour as the regimental one. There were at the outbreak of war three groups of regiments; those with the white (first battalion) Colour, those who were permitted to retain, as a permanent distinction the yellow (second battalion) Colour and those who were awaiting the presentation of new, white Colours.

White regiments were Nos 1, 3, 5 to 38, 40, 42 to 46, 48 to 53, 55, 58 to 80, and all four regiments of Kaiserjäger.

Yellow regiments were Nos 2, 4, 39, 41 and 57.

Awaiting presentation: Nos 47, 54, 81 to 95, 98, 100 and 102.

No Bosnian regiment, Feldjäger battalion or Landwehr unit carried a flag although 10th Feldjäger battalion was permitted to accord to an historic trumpet the same honours as those rendered to a Colour. The proposal to present Colours to Landwehr units had not been carried out before the Great War although each Honved regiment carried one with a distinctive Hungarian design.

The unusual conditions of modern warfare made the carrying of regimental banners under active service conditions a hazardous undertaking and losses to ensigns were unnecessarily high. It was therefore decided that Colours would cease to be carried in action and this proposal was brought into force during 1916.

Colours were of three different designs. The white bore on the one face a representation of the Virgin Mary, outlined in gold and with a corona of twelve silver stars. On the reverse was the Imperial eagle. On the three, free flying sides of the banner was a border $4\frac{3}{4}$ inches deep, made up of red, silver, black and gold flames.

The yellow bore the Imperial eagle on both sides and had the same border as the white Colour.

Honved regimental Colours bore on one face the Arms of Hungary supported by two, winged angels. On the reverse the Royal Monogram together with the words 'Egy Istenem, egy Kiralyom. Ezert halok, azt imadom' (I have one God and one King. For the one I die, to the other I pray). The border of the Honved Colour was made up of alternate red, white and green flames, except in the case of Croatian regiments, where the border triangles were in red, white and blue.

The colour was 132 cms wide and 176 cms long and was flown from a staff 284 cms long. The fourth side of the Colour was wound round the staff and fastened with four rows of gilded nails. Each row of nails fastened a silk band in the colours red, silver, black and gold. The staff head was decorated by a heart-shaped device in gilded metal. Engraved on each side of the device was the Imperial crown and cypher.

The staff was decorated with a bunch of oak leaves and below this were affixed the regimental battle honours and distinctions. These were in the colour of the regimental facings and were worked with either gold or silver thread.

The Imperial eagle which decorated the Colours of Common Army regiments displayed upon its chest and tail the arms of the kingdoms and provinces of the Empire. In the centre of the chest were the arms of Habsburg, Austria and Lorraine. Surrounding that shield were the chains of the knightly orders of the Golden Fleece, St Stephen, Leopold and the Iron Crown, together with the band (red, white, red) of the Maria Theresa Order.

A border of the coats of arms descend to the left and right. On the left the arms of Hungary, Galicia, Lower Austria, Upper Austria, Salzburg and Steiermark. On the right: Bohemia, Istria-Dalmatia, Siebenburgen, Moravia-Silesia and Carinthia-Carniola. Upon the outstretched tail a shield bearing the arms of Tyrol.

Appendix A: Showing Orders of Battle as at August 1914 and October 1918

The main Infantry formations of the Austro-Hungarian Army in August, 1914

The Army's Senior Commander acting on behalf of the Emperor : The Archduke Friedrich

Chief of the General Staff of the Armed Forces : General Conrad von Hötzendorf

Forces for the Balkan theatre of operations

5th Army
VIII Corps (Prague)   XIII Corps (Agram)

6th Army
XV Corps (Sarajevo)   XVI Corps (Ragusa)

2nd Army
IV Corps (Budapest)   VII Corps (Temesvar)   IX Corps (Leitmeritz)

Forces for the Northern theatre of operations

1st Army
I Corps (Cracow)   V Corps (Pressburg)   X Corps (Przemysl)

2nd Army
XII Corps (Hermannstadt)   III Corps (Graz)

3rd Army
XI Corps (Lemberg)   XIV Corps (Innsbruck)

4th Army
II Corps (Vienna)   VI Corps (Kaschau)   XVII Corps

The Balkan Forces

5th Army
VIII Corps (Prague) (26 battalions of Infantry)
9 Infantry Division (Prague)   21 Schützen Division (Prague)
17 Brigade   18 Brigade   41 Brigade   42 Brigade
XIII Corps (Agram) (33 battalions of Infantry)
36 Infantry Division (Agram)   42 Honved Infantry Division (Agram)
71 Brigade   72 Brigade   83 Brigade   13 Infantry Brigade   84 Brigade

6th Army
XV Corps (Sarajevo) (22½ battalions of Infantry)
1 Infantry Division (Sarajevo)   48 Infantry Division
7 Mountain Brigade   9 Mountain Brigade   10 Mountain Brigade   12 Mountain Brigade
XVI Corps (Ragusa) (33½ battalions of Infantry)
18 Infantry Division
4 Mountain Brigade,   5 Mountain Brigade,   6 Mountain Brigade,   8 Mountain Brigade,
1 Mountain Brigade,   2 Mountain Brigade,   13 Mountain Brigade

Under Army command

3 Mountain Brigade
47 Infantry Division (Castelnuova)   14 Mountain Brigade
40 Honved Infantry Division
79 Brigade   80 Brigade

2nd Army

IV Corps (Budapest) (26 battalions of Infantry)
31 Infantry Division (Budapest)   32 Infantry Division (Budapest)
61 Brigade   62 Brigade   63 Brigade   64 Brigade
VII Corps (Temesvar) (28 battalions of Infantry)
17 Infantry Division (Grosswardein)   34 Infantry Division (Temesvar)
33 Brigade   34 Brigade   67 Brigade   68 Brigade
IX Corps (Leitmeritz) (13 battalions of Infantry)
29 Infantry Division (Theresienstadt)
57 Brigade   58 Brigade

Under Army Command

23 Honved Infantry Division (Szegedin)
45 Brigade   46 Brigade
7 Infantry Division
14 Brigade
Banat Area 107 Hungarian Landsturm Brigade

Total of Balkan Forces : $275\frac{1}{2}$ battalions of Infantry
(2nd, Army went from Balkan to Northern theatre during August 1914)

Forces for the Northern theatre of operations

1st Army

I Corps (Cracow) (29 battalions of Infantry)
5 Infantry Division (Olmütz)   46 Schützen Division (Cracow)
9 Brigade   10 Brigade   91 Brigade   92 Brigade
V Corps (Pressburg) (42 battalions)
14 Infantry Division   37 Honved
(Pressburg)   33 Infantry Division   Infantry Division
27 Brigade   28 Brigade   65 Brigade   66 Brigade   73 Brigade   74 Brigade
X Corps (Przemysl) (39 battalions of Infantry)
2 Infantry Division (Jaroslav)   24 Infantry Division (Przemysl)
 3 Brigade   4 Brigade   47 Brigade   48 Brigade
45 Schützen Division
89 Brigade   90 Brigade

Under Army command

12 Infantry Division (Cracow)
23 Brigade   24 Brigade
1 Austrian Landsturm Brigade   36 Austrian Landsturm Brigade
101 Hungarian Landsturm Brigade   110 Austrian Landsturm Brigade
Polish Legion

2nd Army

XII Corps (Hermannstadt) (38 battalions of Infantry)
16 Infantry Division (Hermannstadt)
31 Brigade   32 Brigade
35 Infantry Division   38 Honved Infantry Division
69 Brigade   70 Brigade   75 Brigade   76 Brigade
III Corps (Graz) (45 battalions of Infantry)
6 Infantry Division (Graz)   28 Infantry Division (Laibach)
11 Brigade   12 Brigade   55 Brigade   56 Brigade
22 Schützen Division (Graz)
43 Brigade   44 Brigade

Under Army Command

11 Infantry Division (Lemberg)   43 Schützen Division (Czernowitz)
21 Brigade   22 Brigade   59 Infantry Brigade   86 Schützen Brigade
20 Honved Infantry Division (Grosswardein)
39 Brigade   81 Brigade

3rd Army

XI Corps (Lemberg) (28 battalions of Infantry)
30 Infantry Division
60 Brigade   85 Schützen Brigade   93 Landsturm Infantry Brigade

XIV Corps (Innsbruck) (52 battalions of Infantry)
13 Infantry Division (Linz)   8 Infantry Division (Bolzano)
 5 Brigade   15 Brigade   16 Brigade   96 Brigade   121 Brigade
44 Schützen Division (Innsbruck)
87 Brigade   88 Kaiserschützen Brigade   122 Brigade

Under Army Command

41 Honved Infantry Division
40 Brigade   82 Brigade   97 Hungarian Landsturm Brigade   108 Austrian Landsturm Brigade

4th Army

II Corps (Vienna) (39 battalions of Infantry)
4 Infantry Division (Brünn)   25 Infantry Division (Vienna)
7 Brigade   8 Brigade   49 Brigade   50 Brigade
13 Schützen Division
25 Brigade   26 Brigade
VI Corps (Kaschau) (39 battalions of Infantry)
15 Infantry Division (Miskalco)   27 Infantry Division (Kaschau)
29 Brigade   30 Brigade   53 Brigade   54 Brigade
39 Honved Infantry Division
77 Brigade   78 Brigade
IX Corps (30 battalions of Infantry) : Two divisions of this Corps went to the Northern theatre. One division stayed in the Balkans.
10 Infantry Division (Josefstadt)   26 Schützen Division (Leitmeritz)
19 Brigade   20 Brigade   51 Brigade   52 Brigade
XVII Corps (30½ battalions) Not formed until Augiust 20, 1914
19 Infantry Division (Pilsen)
37 Brigade   38 Brigade
Army Group von Falkenfeld
95 Austrian Landsturm Division (Prague)
106 Austrian Landsturm Division (Olmütz)

Fortress Regiments

Przemysl   97 Hungarian Landsturm Infantry Brigade
                111 Austrian Landsturm Infantry Brigade

Cracow   95 Austrian Landsturm Infantry Brigade
                110 Austrian Landsturm Infantry Brigade

Total forces in the Northern Theatre of Operations 819½ battalions Infantry, 6 cycle companies

Grand Total of the disposition of the Austro-Hungarian Monarchy's Infantry Arm as at August 1914.
1094½ battalions of Infantry : 6 cyclist companies, 1582 machine-gun detachments.
Total number of infantrymen : 1,125,484

The final Order of Battle of the Austro-Hungarian Infantry forces as at 15.10.1918

Supreme Commander : His Majesty The Emperor-King
Chief of the General Staff : Colonel General von Arz

Italian Theatre of Operations

Archduke Joseph's Group of Armies

10th Army
V Corps   XX Corps   XXI Corps   XIV (Edelweiss) Corps

11th Army
III Corps   VI Corps   XIII Corps

Field-Marshal Boroevic's Group of Armies

Army Group Belluno
XXVI Corps   XV Corps   I Corps

6th Army
II Corps   XXIV Corps

The Army of the Isonzo
XVI Corps   IV Corps   VII Corps   XXII Corps   XXIII Corps

The Russian-Rumanian Theatre of Operations

Eastern Army
XXV Corps   XII Corps   XVII Corps

Balkan theatre
XI Corps

Army Group Albania
47 Infantry Division   81 Infantry Division

In France
XVIII Corps Command

Archduke Joseph's Group of Armies

10th Army

V Corps (18 battalions of Infantry)
164 Infantry Brigade   163 Infantry Brigade   22 Schützen Division
                                                 43 Brigade   44 Brigade
XX Corps (24½ battalions of Infantry)
49 Infantry Division   Riva District Troops
97 Brigade   98 Brigade   8 battalions
XXI Corps (13½ battalions of Infantry)
56 Schützen Division
111 Brigade   112 Brigade
XXIV (Edelweiss) Corps (28 battalions of Infantry)
Kaiserjäger Division   19 Infantry Division
1 Brigade   2 Brigade   37 Brigade   38 Brigade
                                                6 Infantry Brigade   159 Infantry Brigade
                                                                      (Army Reserve)

Total strength of 10th Army : 88 battalions of Infantry, 6 Volunteer Rifle battalions, 9 assault battalions, 18 Alpine Companies, 10½ Mountain Guide Companies : 338 machine-gun detachments, 10 half regiments of dismounted cavalry.

Army Group Reserve
(7 battalions of Infantry 3 [Edelweiss] Division)

11th Army

III Corps (23 battalions of Infantry)
6 Infantry Division   52 Infantry Division
11 Brigade   12 Brigade   103 Brigade   104 Brigade
XIII Corps (31 battalions of Infantry)
27 Infantry Division   38 Honved Infantry Division
53 Brigade   54 Brigade   75 Brigade   76 Brigade
                                                31 Infantry Brigade
VI Corps (38 battalions of Infantry)
53 Infantry Division   18 Infantry Division   39 Honved Division
105 Brigade   106 Brigade   35 Brigade   36 Brigade   77 Brigade   78 Brigade

Army Reserve

5 Infantry Division   16 Infantry Division
9 Brigade   10 Brigade   31 Brigade   32 Brigade

Total strength of the 11th Army : 108 battalions of Infantry, 2 Mountain Guide detachments, 25 machine-gun detachments.

Army Group Reserve

36 Infantry Division   74 Honved Division
71 Brigade   72 Brigade   Papp Brigade   Savoly Brigade

Total strength in Infantry of Archduke Joseph's Group of Armies : 220 battalions Infantry, 6 Volunteer Rifle battalions, 9 Assault battalions, 18 Alpine Companies, 12½ Mountain Guide Companies, 363 machine-gun detachments, 30 half regiments of dismounted cavalry.

Field-Marshal Boroevic's Group of Armies

Army Group Belluno

XXVI Corps (42¾ battalions of Infantry)
40 Honved Infantry Division
79 Brigade   80 Brigade
42 Honved Division
83 Brigade   84 Brigade
28 Infantry Division
55 Brigade   56 Brigade
4 Infantry Division
7 Brigade   8 Brigade

I Corps (39 battalions of Infantry)
48 Infantry Division   13 Schützen Division   17 Infantry Division
95 Brigade   96 Brigade   25 Brigade   26 Brigade   33 Brigade   34 Brigade

XV Corps (26 battalions of Infantry)
50 Infantry Division
99 Brigade   100 Brigade
20 Honved Division
39 Brigade   40 Brigade

Army Reserve

(37 battalions of Infantry)
60 Infantry Division   55 Infantry Division   21 Schützen Division
119 Brigade   120 Brigade   109 Brigade   110 Brigade   41 Brigade   42 Brigade

Total of Beullno Army Group : 144¾ battalions of Infantry, 1 Alpine Company

6th Army

II Corps (26 battalions of Infantry)
31 Infantry Division
61 Brigade   62 Brigade
25 Infantry Division
49 Brigade   50 Brigade

XXIV Corps (26 battalions of Infantry)
41 Honved Division
81 Brigade   82 Brigade
51 Honved Division
101 Brigade   102 Brigade

Army Reserve

(30 battalions of Infantry)
10 Infantry Division
19 Brigade   20 Brigade
34 Infantry Division
67 Brigade   68 Brigade
43 Schützen Division
85 Brigade   86 Brigade

Total strength of 6th Army : 83 battalions of Infantry

The Army of Isonzo

XVI Corps (29 battalions of Infantry)
29 Infantry Division   7 Infantry Division   201 Landsturm Brigade
57 Brigade   58 Brigade   13 Brigade   14 Brigade

IV Corps (19 battalions of Infantry)
64 Honved Division
127 Brigade   128 Brigade
70 Honved Division
207 Brigade   208 Brigade

VII Corps (31¾ battalions of Infantry)
33 Infantry Division   12 Infantry Division   24 Infantry Division
65 Brigade   66 Brigade   23 Brigade   24 Brigade   47 Brigade   48 Brigade

XXIII Corps (18 battalions of Infantry)
46 Schützen Division
91 Brigade   92 Brigade
58 Infantry Division
115 Brigade   116 Brigade

XXII Corps (17 battalions of Infantry)
14 Intantry Division
27 Brigade   28 Brigade
2 Infantry Division
3 Brigade   4 Brigade

Army Reserve

(19 battalions of Infantry)
57 Infantry Division
113 Brigade   114 Brigade
26 Schützen Division
51 Brigade   52 Brigade

Total of the Isonzo Army : 133¾ battalions of Infantry, 12 half regiments of dismounted cavalry.

Army Group Reserve

(13 battalions of Infantry)
44 Schützen Division
87 Brigade   88 Brigade

Trieste Area   8 battalions of Infantry
Fiume Area   1¼ battalions of Infantry

Pola Area   5 battalions of Infantry
Gorizia Area   8 battalions of Infantry
Belluno Area $8\frac{1}{4}$ battalions of Infantry

Total of the Boroevic Group of Armies : $388\frac{3}{4}$ battalions of Infantry, 32 half regiments dismounted cavalry, 1 Alpine Company

Russian-Rumanian theatre of operations

Eastern Army

XXV Corps (27 battalions of Infantry)
155 Honved Infantry Division   54 Schützen Division
129 Brigade   130 Brigade   107 Brigade   108 Brigade

XVII Corps ($14\frac{1}{4}$ battalions of Infantry)
11 Infantry Division
21 Brigade   22 Brigade

XII Corps (13 battalions of Infantry)
15 Infantry Division
29 Brigade   30 Brigade

Odessa Government 145 Infantry Brigade

In transit (10 battalions of Infantry)
59 Infantry Division
117 Brigade   118 Brigade

Total of Eastern Army : $66\frac{3}{4}$ battalions of Infantry, 27 half regiments of dismounted cavalry.

16 General Area (under Mackensen's command) (20 battalions of Infantry)
62 Infantry Division
121 Landsturm Brigade   124 Landsturm Brigade
143 Brigade

Various Commands including Bessarabia, General Government of Poland, Siebenburgen. $13\frac{1}{4}$. 33 and 19 battalions of Infantry respectively.

Balkan theatre

XI Corps (in German 11th Army) ($18\frac{1}{2}$ battalions of Infantry)
9 Infantry Division   30 Infantry Division
17 Brigade   18 Brigade   59 Brigade   60 Brigade

Albanian Army Group ($52\frac{3}{4}$ battalions of Infantry)
47 Infantry Division   18 Infantry Division
93 Brigade   94 Brigade   161 Landsturm Brigade
                                     162 Landsturm Brigade
                 220 Landsturm Infantry Brigade

Bosnia, Herzegovina and Dalmatia Command (19 battalions of Infantry)
90 Schützen Brigade   45 Schützen Division

Total of Balkan Theatre troops : 108 battalions of Infantry, 1 Alpine Company, 16 half regiments of dimounted cavalry.

Montenigrian General Government $5\frac{3}{4}$ battalions of Infantry
Serbian General Government   5 battalions of Infantry

In France

XVIII Corps Command ($45\frac{3}{4}$ battalions of Infantry)
106 Infantry Division   1 Infantry Division
210 Landsturm Brigade   1 Brigade   2 Brigade
211 Landsturm Brigade
35 Infantry Division   37 Honved Division
69 Brigade   70 Brigade   73 Brigade   74 Brigade

In Rear Area

32 Infantry Division
63 Brigade   64 Brigade

Appendix B: Regimental numbers, composition and Depots

This appendix gives the number, composition and Depot of the Infantry units of the Austro-Hungarian Army on October 18, 1918.

Not included in the appendix are the Cyclist Battalions, the so called 'Italian' battalions, made up of Italian nationals withdrawn from regiments on the Italian Front; Coastguard Companies, Streif units, Gendarmerie, Military Police, foreign volunteer Legions or independent machine-gun formations.

Common Army Regiments

Number	Nationality	Depot
1	German-Czech	Bennisch
2	Rumanian-Magyar	Prague
3	Czech	Brünn
4	German-Czech	Vienna
5	Magyar-Rumanian	Szatmaremeti
6	Serbo-Croat-German	Pecs
7	German-Slovene	Klagenfurt
8	Czech	Nagyszeben
9	Ruthene	Zuranica near Przemysl
10	Polish-Ruthenian	Neu-Sandec
11	Czech	Gyula
12	Slovak-Magyar	Nagy-Becskerek
13	Polish	Olmütz
14	German	Linz
15	Polish-Ruthenian	Lvov
16	Serbo-Croat	Bjelovar
17	Slovene-Rumanian	Feldbach
18	Czech	Böhm-Leipa
19	Magyar	Körmend
20	Polish	Tarnow
21	Czech	Eger (Hungary)
22	Serbo-Croat	Gyula-Fehervar
23	Magyar-German-Serbo-Croat	Zombor
24	Ruthene	Kolomea
25	Magyar-Slovak	Losoncz
26	Magyar-Slovak	Esztergom
27	German	Graz
28	Czech-Polish	Bruck a/d Mur
29	Mixed	Komoram
30	Polish-Ruthenian	Zamosc
31	German-Magyar-Rumanian	Nowa Padova and Batajnica
32	Magyar	Budapest
33	Rumanian-Magyar-German	Arad
34	Magyar-Slovak	Kassa
35	Czech	Hermagor
36	Czech	
37	Magyar-Rumanian	Hajdubos-Zormeny
38	Magyar-Rumanian	Budapest
39	Magyar-Rumanian	Koniggrätz
40	Polish-Ruthenian	Sternberg (Mähren)
41	Rumanian-Ruthenian-German	Czernovitz
42	German-Czech	Theresienstadt
43	Rumanian-Serbo-Croat	Feher-Tempelon
44	Magyar-German	Kaposvar
45	Polish-Ruthenian	Przemysl-Zasanye
46	Magyar	Bekesc-Saba

47	German-Slovene	Marburg
48	Magyar	Pilsen
49	German	Vienna
50	Rumanian-Magyar	Hodmezo-Vasarhely
51	Rumanian-Magyar	Prague
52	Magyar-German	Budapest
53	Serbo-Croat	Agram
54	Czech-German	Sanok
55	Czech-Ruthenian	Bielitz
56	Polish	Kielce
57	Polish	Prerau
58	Ruthenian-Polish	Lublin
59	German	Salzburg
60	Magyar	Kuttenberg
61	German-Rumanian	Temesvar
62	Magyar-Rumanian	Maros-Vasarhely
63	Rumanian	Koloszvar
64	Rumanian	Vienna
65	Magyar-Ruthenian	Munkacs
66	Magyar-Ruthenian-Slovak	Ungvar
67	Slovak	Eperjos
68	Magyar	Prague
69	Magyar	Pilsen
70	Serbo-Croat	Nagyvarad
71	Slovak	Bestercze
72	Magyar-Slovak	Poszony
73	German	Wrschovitz near Prague
74	Czech-German	Kaaden
75	Czech	Debreczen
76	Magyar-German	Vienna
77	Ruthenian-Polish	Jaroslav
78	Serbo-Croat	Esseg
79	Serbo-Croat	Otocac
80	Ruthenian-Polish	Rimaszombat
81	Czech	Iglau
82	Magyar	Szasvaros
83	Magyar-German	Vienna
84	German	Vienna
85	Ruthenian-Rumanian	Balassa-Gyarmat
86	Magyar-Serb-Croat	Szabadka
87	Slovene	Cilli
88	Czech	Szolnok
89	Ruthenian-Polish	Rzeszov
90	Polish	Jicin
91	German-Czech	Bruck-Kiralyhida
92	German	Komotau
93	German-Czech	Radom
94	German-Czech	Kecskemet
95	Ruthenian-Polish	Stanislau
96	Serbo-Croat	Karlovac
97	Italian-Slovene	Szekes-Fehervar
98	Czech-German	Radkersburg
99	German-Czech-Polish	Znaim
100	Polish-Czech	Piotrkov
101	Magyar	Neuhaus
102	Czech	Hartberg
103	Rumanian-Magyar	Infantry Regiments 63 and 85
104	German	Infantry Regiments 4 and 84
105	Magyar-German	Infantry Regiments 44, 52, 69
106	Magyar-German	Infantry Regiments 83 and 76
107	German	Infantry Regiments 59 and 7
108	Czech-German-Polish	Infantry Regiments 8, 89, 99
109	Ruthenian-Polish	Infantry Regiments 9, 45, 77
110	Polish-Ruthenian	Infantry Regiments 40 and 10
111	Czech	Infantry Regiments 11, 88, 35
112	Magyar-Slovak	Infantry Regiments 71 and 72
113	Polish	Infantry Regiments 13 and 20
114	German	Infantry Regiments 14 and 49
115	Ruthenian-Polish	Infantry Regiments 95 and 15
116	Serbo-Croat	Infantry Regiments 78 and 16
117	Slovene	Infantry Regiments 17, 97, 87
118	Czech	Infantry Regiments 21, 98, 18
119	German-Czech	Infantry Regiments 54, 3, 93
120	Polish-Czech-German	Infantry Regiments 100 and 1

121	German-Czech	Infantry Regiments 94 and 74
122	Serbo-Croat-Slovene	Infantry Regiments 97 and 22
123	Magyar-Serbo-Croat	Infantry Regiments 23 and 86
124	Ruthenian-Polish-German	Infantry Regiments 24, 41, 58
125	Magyar-Slovak	Infantry Regiments 25, 60, 67
126	Magyar-Slovak	Infantry Regiments 12, 19, 26
127	German-Slovene	Infantry Regiments 47 and 27
128	Magyar-Rumanian	Infantry Regiments 62 and 51
129	German-Rumanian	Infantry Regiments 61 and 29
130	Ruthenian-Polish	Infantry Regiments 30, 80, 89
131	Magyar	Infantry Regiments 82 and 31
132	Magyar	Infantry Regiments 68 and 32
133	Magyar-German	Infantry Regiments 33, 46, 101
134	Magyar-Ruthenian-Slovak	Infantry Regiments 34 and 65
135	Serbo-Croat	Infantry Regiments 53 and 96
136	Czech	Infantry Regiments 102, 75, 10
137	German	Infantry Regiments 42 and 92
138	Rumanian-Magyar	Infantry Regiments 50 and 64
139	Magyar-Rumanian	Infantry Regiments 37 and 39
203	(Trachom Regiment)	Infantry Regiments 3, 34, 70, 78
204	(Trachom Regiment) Composite Orient Corps Regiment	Infantry Regiments 45, 86, 78

Tiroler Kaiserjäger Regiments

Number	Nationality	Depot
1	German-Czech	Innsbruck
2	German-Czech	Beneschau
3	German-Czech	Steyr
4	German-Czech	Vöklabruck

Bosnian-Herzegovinian Infantry Regiments

Number	Nationality	Depot
1	Serbo-Croat	Budapest
2	Serbo-Croat	Lebring
3	Serbo-Croat	Budapest
4	Serbo-Croat	Györ
5	Serbo-Croat	1st and 3rd battalions as Bosnian regiment 1 2nd battalion as 5 Bosnian Feldjäger Battalion
6	Serbo-Croat	1st and 2nd battalions as Bosnian regiment 2 3rd battalion as 6 Bosnian Feldjäger Battalion
7	Serbo-Croat	1st and 2nd battalions as Bosnian regiment 3 3rd battalion as 7 Bosnian Feldjäger Battalion
8	Serbo-Croat	1st and 2nd battalions as Bosnian regiment 4 3rd battalion as 8 Bosnian Feldjäger Battalion

Feldjäger Battalions

Number	Nationality	Depot
1	German	Aussig (Elbe)
2	Czech-German	Rozahegy
3	Serbo-Croat	Pancsova

4	Polish	Radynno
5	German	Nowo Radomsk
6	Czech-German	Kaposvar
7	Slovene	Kallwang
8	German-Slovene	Fürnitz (Villach)
9	German	Reichenberg
10	German	St. Pölten
11	Magyar	Györ
12	Czech	Köszeg
13	Polish	Dabrowa
14	Polish-Ruthenian	Przemysl
15	Magyar-Slovak	Löcse
16	German-Czech	Novo Radomsk
17	Czech	Brünn
18	Polish-Ruthenian	Krasnik
19	Magyar-Slovak	Komarom
20	Slovak-Polish	Neumarkt
21	German	Vienna
22	German	Reichenberg
23	Magyar-Ruthenian	Gyoma
24	Magyar	Kiskunhalas
25	Czech-German	Brünn
26	Magyar	Obecse
27	Rumanian-Ruthenian-German	Oaslau
28	Rumanian-Magyar	Kevavara
29	Magyar-Slovak	Losoncz
30	Ruthenian-Polish	Lvov
31	Serbo-Croat	Agram
32	Slovak	Eperjen

Grenzjäger Battalions

1	German-Czech	Infantry Regiment 42
2	German-Czech	Infantry Regiment 1
3	Magyar-Slovak	Infantry Regiment 34
4	Czech-German	Infantry Regiment 54
5	Magyar-Slovak	Infantry Regiment 72
6	Serbo-Croat	Infantry Regiment 16

Bosnian-Herzegovinian Feldjäger Battalions

Number	Nationality	Depot
1	Serbo-Croat	Wiener-Neustadt
2	Serbo-Croat	Judenberg
3	Serbo-Croat	Leoben
4	Serbo-Croat	Knittlefeld
5	Serbo-Croat	Mohacs. Became 2nd battalion 5th Bosnian-Herzeg Regiment
6	Serbo-Croat	Harkany. Became 3rd battalion 6th Bosnian-Herzeg Regiment
7	Serbo-Croat	Siklos. Became 3rd battalion 7th Bosnian-Herzegov Regiment
8	Serbo-Croat	Gyüd. Became 3rd battalion 8th Bosnian-Herzegov Regiment

Hochgebirgs Companies

Number	Nationality	Depot
12	Rumanian-Magyar-German	Infantry Regiment 33
13	German-Polish-Ruthenian	Kaiserschützen Regiment 2
15	German-Czech	Tirolerkaiserjäger Regiment 2
16	Serbo-Croat	Bosnian-Herzeg Infantry Regiment 4
17	German-Ruthenian-Polish	Kaiserschützen Regiment 3
18	German-Ruthenian-Polish	Kaiserschützen Regiment 3
19, 20, 21	German-Polish-Ruthenian	Kaiserschützen Regiment 2
22, 23	German-Czech	Tirolerkaiserjäger Regiment 2
24, 25	German-Czech	Tirolerkaiserjäger Regiment 1
26	German-Czech	Tirolerkaiserjäger Regiment 2
27	German-Czech	Tirolerkaiserjäger Regiment 3
28	German-Polish	Kaiserschützen Regiment 1
29	German-Polish-Ruthenian	Kaiserschützen Regiment 2
30	German-Ruthenian-Polish	Kaiserschützen Regiment 3
31, 32	German-Polish-Ruthenian	Kaiserschützen Regiment 2

Bergführer Companies

Number	Nationality	Depot
1	Mixed	Tirolerkaiserjäger Regiment 1 and Kaiserschützen Regiment 1. Reserve and training Depot at St Christina near Klausen.
2	Mixed	
3	Mixed	
4	Mixed	
5	Mixed	
6	Mixed	
7	Mixed	
8	Mixed	
9	Mixed	
10	Mixed	
11	Mixed	
12	Mixed	
13	Mixed	

Schützen (Landwehr) Regiments

Number	Nationality	Depot
1	German	Vienna
2	German	Brünn
3	German-Czech-Polish	Graz
4	Became Gebirgsschützen Regiment No 1	
5	Italian-Slovene	Voitsberg
6	German	Budweis
7	Czech-German	Rumburg
8	Czech	Salzburg
9	German-Czech	Leitmeritz
10	Czech	Schwaz

Number	Nationality	Depot
11	Czech-German-Polish	Tatatovaros
12	Czech	Nagykanissa
13	Czech-German	Olmütz
14	Czech	Amont
15	German	Cracow
16	Polish	Troppau
17	Polish	Rzeszov
18	Polish-Ruthenian	Przemysl
19	Polish-Ruthenian	Lvov
20	Ruthenian-Polish	Vadovice
21	German	Brünn
22	Ruthenian-Rumanian-German	Czernovitz
23	Serbo-Croat	Orahovica
24	German-Czech	Vienna
25	Czech	St. Pölten
26	Slovene-German	Marburg
27	Became Gebirgsschützen regiment No 2	
28	Czech	Linz
29	German-Czech	Eger (Bohemia)
30	Czech-German	Tulln
31	Polish-Czech	Teschen
32	Polish	Bochnia
33	Ruthenian	Cracow
34	Polish-Ruthenian	Jaroslav
35	Ruthenian-Polish	Sternberg
36	Ruthenian-Polish	Kolomea
37	Serbo-Croat-Czech-Polish	Schärding

Gebirgsschützen Regiments

Number	Nationality	Depot
1	German	Klagenfurt
2	Slovene	Enns

Kaiserschützen Regiments

Number	Nationality	Depot
I	German-Polish	Wels
II	German-Polish-Ruthenian	Laibach
III	German-Ruthenian-Polish	Doboj

Honved Infantry Regiments

Number	Nationality	Depot
1	Magyar-Slovak	Budapest
2	Magyar	Gyula
3	Magyar	Debreczen
4	Magyar-Rumanian	Nagyvarad
5	Magyar	Szeged
6	Serbo-Magyar-German	Szabadka
7	Serbo-Rumanian-German	Versscz
8	Rumanian	Lugos
9	Magyar-Slovak	Kassa

Number	Nationality	Location
10	Magyar-Ruthenian	Miskolcz
11	Magyar-Ruthenian	Jaszbereny
12	Magyar-Rumanian	Eger (Hungary)
13	Slovak-Magyar	Pozsony
14	Slovak-Magyar	Nyitra
15	Slovak	Trencsen
16	Rumanian	Beszterczebanya
17	Magyar	Szekesfehervar
18	Magyar-German	Sopron
19	Magyar-Serbo-Croat	Pecs
20	Magyar	Nagykanizsa
21	Rumanian-Magyar	Kolozsvar
22	Rumanian-Magyar	Maros-Vasahely
23	Rumanian-Magyar	Nagyszeben
24	Rumanian-Magyar	Fogaras
25	Serbo-Croat	Agram
26	Serbo-Croat	Karlovac
27	Serbo-Croat	Sisak
28	Serbo-Croat	Esseg
29	Magyar-Rumanian	Budapest
30	Magyar-Rumanian	Kecskemet
31	Magyar	Veszprem
32	Rumanian-Magyar	Des
300	Rumanian	Honved Regiment No 8
301	Serbo-Rumanian-German	Honved Regiment No 7
302	Magyar	Honved Regiment No 5
305	Magyar	Honved Regiment No 2
306	Magyar-Rumanian	Honved Regiments Nos 23 and 30
307	Magyar-Rumanian-Slovak	Honved Regiments Nos 13 and 23
308	Magyar	Honved Regiments Nos 2 and 10
309	Magyar-Rumanian	Honved Regiments Nos 8, 11, and 18
310	Magyar-Rumanian-German	Honved Regiments Nos 3, 21 and 24
311 (Croat Battalion)	Serbo-Croat	Novo Gradiska
313	Magyar-Rumanian	Honved Regiments Nos 12, 16 and 32
314	Mixed	Honved Regiments Nos 7 and 15
315	Magyar-Rumanian-Slovak	Honved Regiments Nos 4, 9 and 12
316 Trachom (Hungarian battalion)	Rumanian-Magyar	Pecs Honved Regiment No 32

Austrian Landsturm Infantry Regiments
The regimental number agrees with that of the Landsturm Area Command

Number	Nationality
1	German
2	German
6	German-Czech-Polish
9	German
11	Czech-German
13	Czech-Polish-German
16	Polish
22	Ruthenian-Rumanian
23	Serbo-Croat
25	Czech-Polish

26	Slovene
27	Slovene
31	Polish-Ruthenian
32	Polish-Ruthenian
33	Ruthenian
37	Serbo-Croat
39	Czech
51	Polish-German-Czech
409	Czech-German

Austrian Landsturm Infantry Battalions

Number	Nationality	Area Command Number
10	German	3
23	Czech	39
29	Mixed	11
37	German-Czech	24
38	German-Czech	24
39	German-Czech	24
40	German-Czech	25
41	German-Czech	25
42	German-Czech	25
44	German-Czech-Polish	6
45	German-Czech-Polish	6
46	German-Czech-Polish	6
75	German	9
148	Polish-Ruthenian	34
150	German	3
151	German	3
152	German	3
153	German	3
157	German	3
158	Polish	15
159	German-Czech	24
160 to 164	Mixed	I
165 to 169	Mixed	II
170 to 173	Mixed	I
174	German	2
I, II, III and IV Tirol	Mixed	

Hungarian Landsturm Infantry Regiments

Number	Nationality	Depot
1	Magyar-Slovak	Honved Regiment No 1
3	Magyar-Rumanian	Honved Regiments Nos 3, 4, 12
4	Magyar-Rumanian	Honved Regiment No 4
5	Magyar-Rumanian-Slovak	Honved Regiments Nos 5, 14, 21
6	Serbo-Magyar-German	Honved Regiments Nos 6 and 22
8	Rumanian	Honved Regiment No 8
9	Magyar-Slovak	Beszterczbanya
17	Magyar-Slovak	Honved Regiments Nos 1 and 17
19	Rumanian-Magyar-Serb	1st Battalion Honved Regiment 8 2nd and 3rd Battalion Honved Regiment 19 4th Battalion Honved Regiment 29 7th Battalion Honved Regiment 19

20	Magyar-Rumanian	Honved Regiments Nos 22, 23, 31
23	Rumanian-Magyar	Honved Regiment No 23
26	Serbo-Croat	Honved Regiment No 26
29	Magyar-Rumanian	Honved Regiment No 29
30	Magyar-Rumanian	Trencsen
31	Magyar	Trencsen
32	Rumanian-Magyar	Trencsen

Volunteer Rifle Battalions and Companies

Name or Number		Depot
Carinthian	I, II, III battalions	Klagenfurt
Marburg	IV battalion	
Laibach	VI battalion	
Trieste	VII battalion	
Oberösterreich Half battalion		Linz
Salzburg battalion		Salzburg
Steierisches Freiwill. Schützen battalion		Graz
Veteranen Korps Riva-Arco 1 Company		
Österreichisch. Krieger Korps 1 Company		
Deutschmeister Schützen Korps 1 Company		

Tirol and Vorarlberg Standschützen Battalions and Companies

Group or Battalion	Company
1st group	Kitzbuhl : Kufstein-Rattenberg : Schwaz-Zillertal : Auer
2nd group	Landeck : Reutte : Silz-Imst : Feldkirch-Rankweil, Bludenz
Bregenz	Bregenz : Bezau : Dornbirn
Bozen	Bozen : Gries : Sarntheim : Kaltern : Welschnofen
Adige Valley	Klausen : Sterzing : Brizen
Ennenberg	Ennenberg : Groden : Kastelruth
Innsbruck	Innsbruck I : Innsbruck II : Innsbruck III
Merano	Lana : Merano : Passeier : Ulten
Pustertal	Lienz : Sillian : Welsberg
Vintschgau	Glurne : Nauders-Ried : Prad : Schlanders : Taufers-Stilf
—	Cavalese
—	Cles-Male
—	Fassatal
—	Lavarone-Levico
—	Riva-Arco
—	Tione
—	Trient
—	Vallarsa
—	Val Sugana

Appendix C:
Facing and button colours worn by Common Army Infantry regiments

Facing Colour	Button colour			
	Austrian Regiments		Hungarian Regiments	
	Yellow	White	Yellow	White
Dark Red	1	18	52	53
Claret	89	88	—	—
Madder	15	74	44	34
Amaranth	90	95	86	—
Cherry	73	77	43	23
Crimson	84	81	96	82
Scarlet	45	80	37	39
Lobster	35	20	71	67
Pale Red	57	36	65	66
Pink	13	97	5	6
Dark Brown	93	7	12	83
Terra Cotta	55	17	68	78
White	94	92	—	—
Black	14	58	26	28
Orange	59	42	64	63
Gamboge Yellow	27	22	2	31
Sulphur Yellow	99	41	16	101
Steel Green	56	47	48	60
Grass Green	8	28	61	62
Apple Green	9	54	85	79
Seaweed Green	102	—	—	—
Sea Green	21	87	70	25
Parrot Green	91	10	46	50
Sky Blue	4	3	32	19
Light Blue	40	75	72	29
Hazel	100	98	—	—
Pike Grey	30	49	76	69
Ash Grey	11	24	51	33

Note: All Common Army Regiments numbered from 103 upwards wore light blue patches. Herzegovinian regiments wore red. All Shützen, Jäger and Austrian Landsturm wore green. Hungarian Landsturm and Landwehr (Honved) wore slate grey.

Bibliography

Unit histories

Hoen, Seiffert, etc,	Das Deutschmeister Inf. Regiment Nr 4	1928
Kameradschaftsbund der Stei. Frei. Sch.	Die steierisch. freiwilligen Schützen im Felde, 1915-18	Leykam Graz 1935
Raschin	Die Ier Kaiserjäger im Feldzug gegen Russland	Teutsch Bregenz 35
Rost A	Die Kopaljäger im Weltkrieg, 1914-1918. (10th Feldjäger Bn)	Bund der KJ Wien 1938
— —	Das Inr Regiment 99 im Weltkrieg	1929
— —	Heldenweg des Zweier Landsturm	Wimmer. Linz
— —	Das Inf Regiment 94 im Weltkrieg	Reichbg. 1929
— —	Das Standschützen Battalion Bregenz im Weltkrieg	1935
Berndt	Letzter Kampf und Ende der 29 Division	Reichenberg 1928
Saffert E	Mit der Edelweiss Division bis zum Monte Cimone	Gassch. u Luftsc Berlin 1936
Berko	A Magyar Kiralyi Honvedseg Törtenete, 1868-1918	Budapest 1928

Official records

Kriegsarchiv	Österreich-Ungarns Lezter Krieg	Wien 1930
K u K Heer	Instruktionsbuch für die Reserveoffizierschulen; Teil 1 Taktik Teil 2 Waffenwesen Teil 8 Ökonomisch-Admin. Dienst	Wien 1917
K u K Heer	Dienstreglement fur das kuk Heer Teil I : Teil II	Wien 1909/1912
Schmid H von B	Heerwesen Teil 2	Schmid. Wien 1917
War Office	Distribution of the Austro-Hungarian Armies in the Field	War Office 1919
War Office	Handbook of the Austro-Hungarian Army in the Field	War Office June 1918

General

Balek	Development of Tactics—World War	1922
Ö A C	Österreichisch. Aero Club Jahrbuch	Wien 1916
Smith	Mannlicher Rifles and Pistols	1947
Weiss	Mountain training in the former Austro-Hungarian Army	typescript no date
— —	Österreich-Ungarns Heer und Flotte im Weltkrieg	Wien 1923
— —	Feldgrau	Berlin 1956
— —	Illustrirte Geschichte des Weltkrieges	— —